M000032679

Presented To

_____

From

_____

Occasion

_____

Pocket Meditations

Katherine J. Butler

Tyndale House Publishers
Carol Stream, Illinois

LIVING
EXPRESSIONS
COLLECTION

Living Expressions invites you to explore
God's Word in a way that is refreshing to
the spirit and restorative to the soul.

Visit Tyndale online at tyndale.com.

TYNDALE, Tyndale's quill logo, *Living Expressions*, and the Living
Expressions logo are registered trademarks of Tyndale House
Publishers.

Pocket Meditations

Copyright © 2020 by Ronald A. Beers. All rights reserved.

Cover and interior illustrations by Lauren Lowen. Copyright © 2020 by
Tyndale House Publishers. All rights reserved.

Designed by Jackie Nuñez

Scripture quotations are taken from the *Holy Bible*, New Living
Translation, copyright © 1996, 2004, 2015 by Tyndale House
Foundation. Used by permission of Tyndale House Publishers, Carol
Stream, Illinois 60188. All rights reserved.

For information about special discounts for bulk purchases, please
contact Tyndale House Publishers at csresponse@tyndale.com, or call
1-800-323-9400.

ISBN 978-1-4964-1812-8

Printed in China

26   25   24   23   22   21   20
7   6   5   4   3   2   1

Introduction

WHETHER YOU'RE NEW TO THE BIBLE or have been immersing yourself in its message for years, the same wonderful truth applies: You will reap eternal benefits each time you meditate on its timeless wisdom.

As you begin your journey through *Pocket Meditations*, keep in mind that we all meditate on something at various points throughout each day. To meditate is to focus your thought and attention on one particular matter. For some, it might mean contemplating schedules or agendas. For others, it may involve thinking deeply about current worries or getting bogged down with past regrets or failures.

While the word *meditation* has some unfortunate baggage these days, the practice is actually essential to the Christian faith. We must think deeply about God's

Word—reflecting on what it says about him and pondering what it reveals about us and our world. We cannot internalize the truths of God unless we slow down and ingest them.

The concept of meditation is mentioned throughout the Bible: Joshua said we should meditate on God's law "day and night" (Joshua 1:8). David prayed that his meditations would be pleasing to God (Psalm 19:14). Meditation is also mentioned in several psalms (48:9; 63:6; 119; 145:5).

What do you meditate on most often? How might your life be different if each day you chose to pause and meditate on God's Word? This book is designed to help you do that. Every page provides a well-known and inspirational passage from God's Word as well as a devotional thought to prompt you to meditate more deeply on its message.

Here are a few tips before you begin:

1. Read (and reread) each Bible passage *slowly*. God's Word cannot sink into your heart through skimming. Take a breath before you read, and then allow your mind to settle on each verse.

2. Give yourself grace. It's hard to stay still and focused. That's why meditation is considered a discipline! If distractions arise, remind yourself that replacing old thoughts with new ones takes time. Let go of preoccupations as best you can in order to engage with the Scriptures.

3. Remember that you are reading God's Word, which is "*alive* and *powerful*" (Hebrews 4:12, emphasis added). It always produces fruit. You may not feel any different in the moment, but trust that God will accomplish great work in you through these meditations.

God bless you as you think deeply about his Word, his character, and his presence in your life!

Genesis 1:1

*In the beginning God created
the heavens and the earth.*

The first five words of the Bible reveal so
much to us about God: "In the beginning God
created." God's Word begins by affirming
that he existed before anything else and that
he alone brought all things into existence.
He didn't use other materials to form the
heavens and the earth; he created all things
from nothing. This concept is almost impossible
for us to grasp, yet it reminds us of his
power, sovereignty, and wisdom. If God is able
to speak all things into existence, how much
more can he be trusted to handle the impossible
areas in your own life?

Genesis 1:27

God created human beings in his own image.
In the image of God he created them;
male and female he created them.

To be created in God's image means we
resemble God—in our ability to create, reason, rule over animals, and be in relationship.
How amazing it is that God didn't create us to
be his puppets but to resemble and represent
him in this world! How often do you thank
God for seeing you as worthy to share his
image? Since God treasures you this much,
surely he has something important for you to
do in this world.

Psalm 1:1-3

Oh, the joys of those who do not follow the advice of the wicked, or stand around with sinners, or join in with mockers. But they delight in the law of the Lord, meditating on it day and night. They are like trees planted along the riverbank, bearing fruit each season. Their leaves never wither, and they prosper in all they do.

The book of Psalms begins by stressing the importance of obeying the law—God's Word. This passage contrasts a life of delighting in the Word of God against a life of following one's own way. Which most resembles your own? Do you come to Scripture for advice or rely solely on human wisdom? Does it seem that you are fruitful and thriving or dry and withering? Ask God for help in learning to love his Word as you continue through this devotional.

Genesis 18:14

Is anything too hard for the LORD?

Abraham, who was nearly one hundred years old, and his ninety-year-old wife, Sarah, were childless when God told Abraham the unexpected news that Sarah would finally have a child. Imagine living that long without seeing a deep desire of your heart come to fruition. Sarah's hope for a child had likely dwindled with each year that passed until at last she deemed it impossible, laughing at the prospect. But God responded, "Is anything too hard for the LORD?" These words combat despair, hopelessness, and pessimism. They remind us that God can do anything—yes, *anything.* God sees the desires of your heart. He knows the pain and helplessness you feel because of that impossible situation in your life. What might God want you to keep hoping for as you choose to trust him with the impossible?

Genesis 24:7

The LORD, the God of heaven . . . will send his angel ahead of you.

Abraham decided to send his most trusted servant on a long journey to find a wife for his son Isaac. Before the servant left, Abraham told him, "God . . . will send his angel ahead of you." God clearly showed his love and care for this servant by sending an angel ahead to help him on his journey. Do you long for this in your own life—someone to walk ahead of you to prepare your path? Whatever situation you are about to walk into, pray that God will send an angel ahead of you. Trust that he cares for you in the same way he cared for Abraham's servant.

Genesis 50:20

You intended to harm me, but God intended it all for good.

Abraham's great-grandson, Joseph, spoke these words to his brothers after enduring a long, painful history with them. They had plotted to kill him because he was their father's favorite child. Thankfully they changed their minds and sold him into slavery instead, yet they lied to their father about his fate. Years later, Joseph came face-to-face with his brothers again, but this time he was the one in power and chose to forgive them. After their father died, his brothers were still afraid of retribution from Joseph and fell down before him, begging for forgiveness. When Joseph answered them with the words in this passage, it demonstrated that God is able to use *anything*—even human sin—to bring about good. If you have been harmed, or if you have regretfully harmed another, take comfort in remembering this.

Psalm 3:3-4

You, O LORD, are a shield around me; you are my glory, the one who holds my head high. I cried out to the LORD, and he answered me from his holy mountain.

David wrote this beautiful psalm during a time of turmoil, when one of his own sons had turned against him. Even though it begins with despair, it quickly turns into a psalm filled with hope. Our earthly troubles often sweep us toward a black hole of anguish, but David's words remind us to look back up to our Creator. He is the one who "holds our heads high" when our strength and hope have been depleted. What is keeping you from lifting your face toward God today? Whatever it is, be encouraged that your heavenly Father is your shield, your protector, and your helper. He listens to your cries, and he promises to answer.

Exodus 4:11-13

The LORD asked Moses, "Who makes a person's mouth? Who decides whether people speak or do not speak, hear or do not hear, see or do not see? Is it not I, the LORD? Now go! I will be with you...." But Moses again pleaded, "Lord, please! Send anyone else."

Have you ever argued with God, begging him to choose someone else for a task that you feel unequipped for? Moses had just informed God that he wasn't a polished speaker, so he couldn't confront Pharaoh, Egypt's king, and demand freedom from slavery for the Israelites. Yet God reminded Moses that *he* was the one who had created his mouth and would be with him to help him speak. In what areas do you feel inadequate? How might God want to work through your insecurity to show his great power?

Exodus 14:13-14

Moses told the people, "Don't be afraid. Just stand still and watch the LORD rescue you today. . . . The LORD himself will fight for you."

After the Egyptians had endured ten plagues brought upon them by the Lord, Pharaoh finally released the Israelites. But soon after, Pharaoh changed his mind and commanded his army to chase them down and bring them back into captivity. The Israelites were in an impossible situation—caught between Pharaoh's army and the Red Sea—when Moses spoke his reassuring words. We all experience times when life feels hopeless and there seems to be no way out. When we don't know what to do, these words give us direction and hope in the midst of despair: *Don't be afraid. Be still. Watch for the Lord. He will fight for you and rescue you.* Do you need to be reminded of this promise today?

Proverbs 1:7

Fear of the LORD is the foundation of true knowledge, but fools despise wisdom and discipline.

Fearing God begins with knowing who he is and who we are. He is powerful and mighty, yet loving and merciful. He is the maker of the heavens and earth—and us! Therefore true knowledge begins with humility and respect for our Creator. Wisdom comes when we trust God's instructions for how to view the world and ourselves. Proverbs 1:7 describes as "fools" those who believe their own wisdom and insights are better than God's. This thought sets the stage for the rest of the book of Proverbs, which contrasts the joy of trusting and following God's way with the sorrow that comes from trusting our own way.

Exodus 15:2-3

The LORD is my strength and my song; he has given me victory. This is my God, and I will praise him—my father's God, and I will exalt him! The LORD is a warrior; Yahweh is his name!

The Israelites had just witnessed their own miraculous rescue by the Lord. He parted the Red Sea, led them safely across the dry seabed, and caused the water to swallow up Pharaoh and his entire army as it crashed back into place. Then everyone sang a song of praise to God. This passage from the song reveals so much about God's character: He is strong, he is a warrior, he fights evil on our behalf, and he will always be victorious. This is the kind of God we serve. You can bravely face your day knowing that the God who parted the Red Sea is on your side.

Exodus 34:29

When Moses came down Mount Sinai carrying the two stone tablets inscribed with the terms of the covenant, he wasn't aware that his face had become radiant because he had spoken to the LORD.

Moses spent forty days on a mountaintop with God. When he came down, his face was radiant—not because of anything he had done, but simply because he had spent time in God's presence. Have you ever been in the presence of someone you knew had recently spent time with God? Maybe you noticed that person's peace, joy, or thankful heart, or simply their capacity to love you well. This is what God offers to those who are intentional in their time with him. Even if you can spend only four minutes reading his Word or forty seconds praying, take those moments and experience the radiant joy that comes from being in his presence.

15

Leviticus 26:3, 11-13

If you follow my decrees and are careful to obey my commands, . . . I will live among you. . . . I will walk among you; I will be your God, and you will be my people. I am the LORD your God.

In Leviticus 26:1-13, God reveals some of the blessings that come to those who faithfully follow him. One of the greatest blessings they receive is the visible expression of his presence. When we choose to step out in faith and respond to God's calling, we suddenly see evidence of him working on our behalf. When we give generously, especially when it hurts, we see his faithful provision. When we make time for him every day, we experience him aligning our hearts and minds with his perfect law. How might God be calling you toward obedience in a specific area of your life?

Psalm 18:31-33, 36

Who is God except the LORD? Who but our God is a solid rock? God arms me with strength, and he makes my way perfect. He makes me as sure-footed as a deer, enabling me to stand on mountain heights. . . . You have made a wide path for my feet to keep them from slipping.

Time and again Scripture reminds us that God empowers his children with unique and divine strength. Perhaps he knew we would need plenty of it during our time in this world. Life has its share of problems and scary situations. But whatever we face, God's Word reassures us that he is stronger than our greatest problems. He is our "solid rock." When the earth feels like it's moving underneath you, stand on this truth: God is your strength. Hold tight to him, and he will keep you from slipping.

Numbers 6:24-26

May the LORD bless you and protect you. May the LORD smile on you and be gracious to you. May the LORD show you his favor and give you his peace.

Called the "Aaronic Blessing," this passage, which God commanded the high priest, Aaron, and his sons to speak over the people of Israel, is one of the most famous blessings in the Bible. In Scripture, blessing someone is a profoundly personal and powerful act. When we bless others, we're asking God to bring about good things in their lives. Throughout the Bible we often see people speaking blessings over others. This beautiful practice is one that is often forgotten in our churches and homes today. Whom might God be asking you to bless? Someone you mentor? Your child? Maybe even an enemy? Ask him to make you aware of the next opportunity to speak forth encouraging, life-giving words.

Deuteronomy 4:9

Be careful never to forget what you yourself have seen. Do not let these memories escape from your mind as long as you live! And be sure to pass them on to your children and grandchildren.

The Israelites had a tendency to forget the wonderful things God had done for them. But don't we all tend to forget or ignore the good things God has done in our lives, or at least move on too quickly? God knows we are prone to forgetfulness, and he has often reminded his people to remember his kind acts. In addition, he said we are responsible to tell the next generation about his faithfulness. What has God recently done for you? How can you be more intentional in recalling the wonderful stories of his care and passing them along to those who come after you?

Psalm 19:14

May the words of my mouth and the meditation of my heart be pleasing to you, O LORD, my rock and my redeemer.

Psalm 19 is a beautiful song written by David, praising God for revealing himself to us through his world and his Word. He ends the song with a prayer that his words and thoughts would be pleasing to the Lord. We often speak our minds without thinking about the consequences of our words. How would our days be different if we began them with this same plea? What would it be like to be more intentional about what we think and more discerning about what we say? How might it impact our relationships? Take a moment to read this great verse of the Bible aloud as a prayer for today.

Deuteronomy 6:5

Love the LORD your God with all your heart, all your soul, and all your strength.

God calls each of us to exclusive and complete devotion to him. Is your heart set on God? What are you doing to keep your focus on him? Do you give energy and priority to knowing him more each day? Giving God first place isn't easy, but it *is* life changing! The world is constantly demanding our attention, pulling us away from time with God. Choose today to take a step toward loving God well by opening your heart to him in prayer, filling your mind with words from Scripture, and loving others "as yourself" (Matthew 22:39). You will never regret spending time growing in knowledge of and love for your Creator.

Deuteronomy 33:26-27

There is no one like the God of Israel. He rides across the heavens to help you, across the skies in majestic splendor. The eternal God is your refuge, and his everlasting arms are under you.

At the end of the book of Deuteronomy, Moses gave his final blessing to Israel before his death. Imagine the weight of words spoken by someone who is about to pass on; most likely they will be some of the most important they have ever spoken. Moses chose to emphasize to God's people that there is *no one* like God, who comes from heaven to help us, and that he is our refuge and holds us in his arms for all eternity. Did you need to hear those words today? Take these great verses of the Bible to heart and meditate on them often. These words are for you too!

Joshua 1:9

This is my command—be strong and courageous! Do not be afraid or discouraged. For the LORD your God is with you wherever you go.

In this verse, the Lord commissioned Joshua to lead the people of Israel. How much pressure might Joshua have experienced as Moses' successor? When God calls us to a big task, he enables us to do it with strength and courage. Perhaps you are facing an undertaking that feels far beyond your abilities. God speaks these empowering words of encouragement to you too: *Do not be afraid. Do not let discouragement keep you from doing a job well. Don't give up.* God is with you and has promised to neither fail you nor leave you to accomplish this task alone. Take it one day at a time and trust that he will be with you every step of the way.

Proverbs 2:1, 3-6

*Listen to what I say, and treasure my commands.
. . . Cry out for insight, and ask for understanding.
Search for them as you would for silver;
seek them like hidden treasures. Then you will
understand what it means to fear the LORD,
and you will gain knowledge of God. For the LORD
grants wisdom! From his mouth come
knowledge and understanding.*

Every person has an area in life that requires delicate care—maybe a conflict at work, a difficult family relationship, or a big financial decision. These verses in Proverbs offer a great promise: When we consistently tap into God's unlimited knowledge, we receive divine wisdom to help us navigate the challenges of daily life. Ask God what he wants you to do; then listen to his voice through his Word and treasure his advice. God promises wisdom to those who are intentional with him.

Joshua 24:14-15

Serve the LORD alone. But if you refuse to serve the LORD, then choose today whom you will serve. . . . As for me and my family, we will serve the LORD.

In these verses, Joshua is urging the nation of Israel to let go of their idols and serve God alone. Idolatry isn't just a problem the Israelites faced; it's an issue every human heart struggles with. When we depend on something other than God to meet a need deep inside us, we are worshiping an idol. Joshua sternly warned God's people to examine their hearts and choose whom they would serve. What things are you tempted to use to fill the holes in your heart? Perhaps money? Food? Success? Material possessions? Have an honest conversation with God about them as a first step to committing yourself and your household to serving God alone.

Judges 6:12, 14, 16

Mighty hero, the LORD is with you!... Go with the strength you have.... I am sending you!... I will be with you.

God called Gideon to save the nation of Israel from the cruelty of the Midianites, even though Gideon's clan was the weakest in his tribe and he was the least influential in his household. The Bible is full of people who felt reluctant and unqualified to carry out the tasks God had called them to. Whenever you feel weak, fearful, underqualified, or incapable, remember that God is speaking over you these same words he spoke to Gideon. Use whatever strength you have toward the task, and it will be enough. You can be sure that if God asks you to do something for him, he will demonstrate his great power through you.

Psalm 27:1

*The LORD is my light and my salvation—
so why should I be afraid? The LORD is my
fortress, protecting me from danger, so
why should I tremble?*

So many passages in the Bible both
encourage and command us not to
be afraid. This particular verse on
fear has a different spin: It poses the
question, "Why should I be afraid?"
Why should we fear circumstances
that come our way when God is
our light here on earth and has
promised us a home in heaven when
we die? This Scripture provides an
eternal perspective by reminding us
that God is our ever-present, loving
protector. Ask yourself today, *What
do I really need to be afraid of if this
is the kind of God I serve?*

Ruth 1:16

Wherever you go, I will go; wherever you live,
I will live. Your people will be my people,
and your God will be my God.

When famine struck Israel, Naomi and her
family moved to a foreign country, where
Naomi's sons married. Sadly, Naomi and her
daughters-in-law eventually became wid-
ows. After the famine in Israel ended, Naomi
decided to return to her homeland. But on
the way, Naomi urged Orpah and Ruth to go
back to their country. Orpah decided to leave,
but Ruth would not. Ruth's decision to care
for her mother-in-law not only threatened
her chances to remarry and have children
but also meant leaving her people and their
gods. Later God blessed Ruth for her selfless-
ness by giving her a new husband and a baby.
No sacrifice you make for another will go
unnoticed by God. He loves to bless those who
put others first.

1 Samuel 3:9

Speak, LORD, your servant is listening.

God called to Samuel, a young boy, three times one night, but Samuel didn't recognize his voice. Then Eli the priest realized the Lord had been speaking. Eli told Samuel that if the Lord called a fourth time, he should say, "Speak, LORD, your servant is listening." Samuel didn't know the Lord before this, but how often do we who already know him push through life without listening for his guidance? How many times has he called us but we've failed to recognize his voice? How often do we pray but neglect to wait quietly for God's answer? How often do we come to God with our own agendas instead of asking for his? Take time to be still before God so you can pray these six simple words. If God has something to say, you don't want to miss it.

1 Samuel 16:7

*The LORD doesn't see things the way you see them.
People judge by outward appearance,
but the LORD looks at the heart.*

Samuel grew up to be a prophet, and when God led him to anoint one of Jesse's sons as Israel's next king, Jesse presented Eliab. Because of Eliab's looks, Samuel thought he was God's chosen leader. But the Lord reminded Samuel not to judge based on appearance. Jesse didn't summon his youngest son, David, until the Lord had rejected Jesse's other sons. But God had seen David's heart and decided he was the best man for the job. How often do you miss out on gaining potential friends or hiring great employees because you've been conditioned to think that those with power, money, or influence make good leaders? Ask God to help you see the hearts of others instead of judging them by their appearance.

Psalm 27:4

The one thing I ask of the LORD—the thing I seek most—is to live in the house of the LORD all the days of my life.

Good hospitality is an act of love because it involves sharing your space, time, resources, and presence. These words from the book of Psalms give us a beautiful picture of how God does the same for us. Even though David was singing this psalm as praise to God, it is a good reminder that we who love God will also be welcomed into his home when we leave this earth. Imagine the rest, security, and delight you will feel living in the Lord's house with him, knowing that no circumstance will take you away. Use this picture as motivation and encouragement to stay close to the Lord today.

1 Samuel 17:45

You come to me with sword, spear, and javelin, but I come to you in the name of the LORD of Heaven's Armies.

This verse comes from the famous story of David and Goliath. Goliath was a great Philistine giant and an intimidating champion whom everyone feared. He had picked a fight with God's nation of Israel, and therefore with God himself. Because of David's strong and vibrant faith, he was determined not to allow Goliath to defy his God. Even though the odds seemed stacked against him, David spoke these words to Goliath moments before he defeated him. Whatever enemies, weapons, or circumstances are pitted against you today, remember this: Your greatest advantage is having the Lord of Heaven's Armies on your side. Come to him and trust that he will help you with the impossible.

32

1 Chronicles 16:23-25

Let the whole earth sing to the LORD!
Each day proclaim the good news that
he saves. Publish his glorious deeds
among the nations. Tell everyone about
the amazing things he does. Great is the
LORD! He is most worthy of praise!

David presented this song of praise after the Ark of the Covenant had finally been transported safely to Jerusalem. This was a major event in the history of the Israelites that was cause for celebration, for the Ark of the Covenant not only carried the tablets with the Ten Commandments but also served as an important symbol of God's presence. These verses offer specific ways we can celebrate God's presence and goodness in our own lives: *singing* to the Lord, *proclaiming* his salvation, *publishing* his deeds, and *telling* everyone about what he has done. How can you celebrate today what God has done for you?

Proverbs 3:5-6

Trust in the LORD with all your heart;
do not depend on your own understanding.
Seek his will in all you do, and he will
show you which path to take.

A theme throughout Proverbs is that the fear of God is the beginning of wisdom. Fearing God involves knowing who he is and who we are in relation to him. He is our Creator and we are his creation; therefore he knows what is best for our lives. Most everyone can relate to the uneasy feeling of releasing control to something or someone other than ourselves. Yet God promises that when we forfeit our own agendas and believe he will help us with the challenges and unknowns of daily life, he will show us the right direction to take. What are some practical ways in which you can seek God's will "in all you do"?

1 Chronicles 28:9-10

Learn to know the God of your ancestors intimately. Worship and serve him with your whole heart and a willing mind. For the Lord sees every heart and knows every plan and thought. If you seek him, you will find him.... The Lord has chosen you.... Be strong, and do the work.

David was giving these specific instructions to his son Solomon before he anointed him as Israel's next king. You would think the instructions handed down from one king to the next would be about maintaining power, wealth, and property. Yet David's focus was solely on Solomon's relationship with the Lord because he knew this was more important than anything else. What a beautiful reminder for us as well. When we seek to know God intimately and serve him with everything we have, the events of our lives work together for his glory and our good.

2 Chronicles 7:14-15

If my people who are called by my name will humble themselves and pray and seek my face and turn from their wicked ways, I will hear from heaven and will forgive their sins. . . . My eyes will be open and my ears attentive to every prayer.

The Lord appeared to Solomon with specific instructions for how his people could develop a right relationship with him: First, they needed to humble themselves and pray, acknowledging their sins. It's hard to admit when we've done something wrong, but it is the first step to a restored relationship with God. Second, they had to turn from sinful actions toward God's way of living. This is *repentance*, which literally means "to turn." Humility paves the way to a restored relationship with God and others. A restored relationship is one of the most powerful demonstrations of real love.

2 Chronicles 16:9

The eyes of the LORD search the whole earth in order to strengthen those whose hearts are fully committed to him.

Though Hanani, a prophet, spoke this verse to King Asa of Judah thousands of years ago, it remains relevant today. Hanani had just rebuked Asa for seeking help from a foreign king instead of from God. Hanani reminded Asa that the Lord is always watching and assessing people's hearts (their motives) with the intent of strengthening those committed to him. Even when it seems like God doesn't see you, trust that he knows every heart and will strengthen those devoted to following him. Let this encourage you to press on in faithfulness today.

Psalm 31:7

I will be glad and rejoice in your unfailing love, for you have seen my troubles, and you care about the anguish of my soul.

David was crying out to God about the troubles his enemies had caused him. Even though he was in deep distress, he was able to be glad and praise God for caring about his misery. Have you ever felt alone in your pain? Maybe it was difficult to believe that God cared about what you were going through. This verse offers comforting truths for those whose souls are in anguish: *God loves you. He sees you. And he cares for you in your pain. You can rejoice in this!*

2 Chronicles 20:15, 17

Do not be afraid! Don't be discouraged . . .
for the battle is not yours, but God's. . . .
You will not even need to fight. . . . Stand still
and watch the LORD's victory.
He is with you.

A great army was about to invade the nation of Judah. God's people were outnumbered, unprepared, and terrified. Then Jahaziel gave this prophecy from the Lord, commanding them not to be afraid, because they wouldn't even need to fight. Sometimes God calls us to step forward in an act of trust; at other times, he asks us to trust him by staying put. Are you facing a battle that feels too big to handle? Ask God if he wants you to take action or stand still and watch him intervene on your behalf. Do not be afraid or discouraged, for God is with you.

Ezra 7:28

I felt encouraged because the gracious hand of the
LORD my God was on me.

Three times in Ezra 7 we find a variation of
the phrase "The gracious hand of the LORD
was on [Ezra]." Earlier in the chapter we
discover exactly why God chose to show Ezra
so much favor: "Because Ezra had determined
to study and obey the Law of the LORD and to
teach [it] to the people" (verse 10). There are
few things we should want more than God's
favor, because receiving his favor means
we are in a healthy relationship with him.
Whatever good comes to us is because God
graciously chooses to give it. And as we dedi-
cate ourselves to studying and obeying his
Word, it becomes very clear what kind of life
honors him most and puts us in a position to
receive more favor from him.

Psalm 31:14-16

But I am trusting you, O Lord, saying, "You are my God!" My future is in your hands.... Let your favor shine on your servant."

Do you long to speak these words from a sincere heart? How might your life be different if you could say and act on these words with confidence? Maybe you wouldn't be up at night worrying about the future. Or perhaps you would live more bravely, speaking out for justice and goodness. Or maybe you would experience joy believing God has your future in his caring hands. Whatever worries are weighing on your heart today, recite these verses as a prayer. Remember this truth during the day and fall asleep with it on your mind. God is able (and wants!) to change your thoughts, actions, and heart through his Word.

Nehemiah 8:10, 12

*Go and celebrate with a feast of rich foods and
sweet drinks.... So the people went away to
eat and drink ... and to celebrate with great joy
because they had heard God's words and
understood them.*

Ezra had just read God's laws to a large
group of people. Many listened carefully
and repented of their sins. Then Ezra told
them to celebrate! Celebration is about
calling attention to something important so
it can be remembered. It is closely linked to
gratitude because it involves pausing to be
grateful for something the Lord has done.
Sometimes we celebrate wonderful events
like the birth of a child or a wedding, and
other times we celebrate when we've perse-
vered through painful seasons. What is one
thing you want to celebrate from the past
year? How can you weave gratitude into
your celebration?

Esther 4:14

If you keep quiet at a time like this, deliverance and relief for the Jews will arise from some other place, but you and your relatives will die. Who knows if perhaps you were made queen for just such a time as this?

When God's people were exiles in Persia, a young woman named Esther found favor with the king and was chosen to be queen. After she learned of a plot to destroy her people, she faced a dilemma: Either risk her life to save them or remain silent to spare her own, for approaching the king without an invitation was punishable by death. Then Mordecai, Esther's relative, suggested that perhaps this situation was the whole reason Esther was made queen. God puts people in places and positions for a reason; how might he be using your location, influence, or abilities for "such a time as this"?

Job 1:21

The LORD gave me what I had,
and the LORD has taken it away.
Praise the name of the LORD!

For those who have lost someone
or something of great worth, these
words are hard to read. A man
named Job spoke them after learning he had lost everything. Before
this happened, Job had everything
a person could ever want, including
a beautiful family. God allowed his
enemy, Satan, to test Job's character,
so Satan took away all of Job's possessions. Yet Job's response to grief
shows his great character, his abso-
lute devotion to God, and his trust
that God would eventually make
things right. Satan intended for Job
to turn his back on God, but Job
chose to praise God's name instead.
How might Job's response encourage you to turn toward God in your
seasons of loss?

Proverbs 3:27-28

Do not withhold good from those who deserve it when it's in your power to help them. If you can help your neighbor now, don't say, "Come back tomorrow, and then I'll help you."

The book of Proverbs advises us how to live wisely. In our culture, we think wise living is self-focused; how can I make the most out of *my* life? How do I make decisions that will most benefit *me*? But the Bible focuses on how to live a life focused on helping *others*. For those who have chosen to follow God, this radical others-centered lifestyle is expected of us, because it demonstrates that we understand what real love looks like. We are commanded to not withhold good from others and to help whenever possible. Is your focus on living wisely? Are you living for your own sake or for the good of those around you?

Job 9:32-33, 35

God is not a mortal like me, so I cannot argue with him or take him to trial. If only there were a mediator between us, someone who could bring us together. . . . Then I could speak to him without fear, but I cannot do that in my own strength.

After Job had lost everything, his friends came to sit with him in his grief. Unfortunately, they weren't the best comforters; they suggested he had done something wrong to deserve his suffering. This passage includes part of his response. What Job wished for is exactly what God was planning to do, for centuries later, God sent Jesus, the perfect mediator "who pleads our case before the Father" (1 John 2:1). Because of Jesus, we can now draw near to God without fear. Will you let these truths encourage you to talk to God today?

Ecclesiastes 3:11

God has made everything beautiful for its own time. He has planted eternity in the human heart, but even so, people cannot see the whole scope of God's work from beginning to end.

The writer of the book of Ecclesiastes is telling his story about struggling to find meaning in life. This verse says that because God placed an eternal soul in every person he created, we long for something more than what this world has to offer. We instinctively know that we were made for an eternal purpose. The beauty we see around us may give us a sense of wonder and satisfaction in the moment, but these feelings point to something even greater and more lasting: our Creator and the eternal home we will one day share with him. Allow this truth to help you make the most of your life today.

Psalm 32:8

The LORD says, "I will guide you along the best pathway for your life. I will advise you and watch over you."

As we journey through life, we face many tough decisions. These situations bring up questions like *How do I know which way God wants me to go? Does he have a perfect plan for my life? What happens if I make the wrong choice?* No matter what scary unknowns loom ahead, God promises to guide us along the best path. However, he wants us to first ask him for advice. In what situation do you need God's wisdom? Where do you need direction? Ask God for his guidance and remind yourself of this comforting verse from his Word.

Isaiah 1:18

"Come now, let's settle this," says the LORD. "Though your sins are like scarlet, I will make them as white as snow. Though they are red like crimson, I will make them as white as wool."

This beautiful verse reminds us that God pursues us—even in our worst moments. Even though God's people had forsaken him, he kept calling them back to himself, longing for reconciliation. But it could occur only if they first made a deliberate choice to recognize the wrong they had done. Perhaps God wants to settle something with you as well—maybe it has to do with an attitude that needs to be changed or an idol that has taken root in your life. If so, talk about it with the Lord and remember that no matter how badly sin has stained your life, God has promised to make you clean again.

Isaiah 26:3-4

You will keep in perfect peace all who trust in you, all whose thoughts are fixed on you! Trust in the LORD always, for the LORD GOD is the eternal Rock.

This beautiful verse promises that all who focus on loving and following God will experience his perfect peace. Our world is full of people who struggle with anxiety, fear, and worry, fixing their thoughts on things they cannot control. But what would it be like to feel perfectly at peace? We can find this peace by directing our anxious thoughts back to God and deliberately filling our minds with his Word when we feel afraid. God's Word describes him as "the eternal Rock." Leaning on him gives us stability and security as we trust him to hold us up. And as we rest against him, we "experience God's peace, which exceeds anything we can understand" (Philippians 4:7).

Isaiah 40:8

*The grass withers and the flowers fade,
but the word of our God stands forever.*

When the Babylonians were holding
God's people captive, Isaiah offered
them comfort with this prophecy.
But this verse was written not only
for the people of Judah thousands
of years ago; it is the recorded Word
of God and one of the main ways
he speaks to us today. God's Word
is living, reliable, everlasting, and
never-failing. No matter how much
this world changes, the truth of
God's Word never will. And no matter what season of life you are in,
God has something to say to you.
Ask him to give you an open heart to
receive whatever he wants to reveal
to you through his Word.

Psalm 34:8-9

Taste and see that the LORD is good.
Oh, the joys of those who take refuge in him!
Fear the LORD, you his godly people,
for those who fear him will have all they need.

In this psalm, David was expressing his thanks to God for taking care of him and protecting him. Because of his experience, he encouraged others to "taste," or experience, the goodness of the Lord. Do you long to have a taste of God's goodness today? You can experience it by asking him for protection and trusting him to take care of your needs. As you do, let your mind dwell on two truths: Those who take refuge in God will experience joy and an eternal relationship with him, and those who fear God will have everything they truly need in life.

Isaiah 40:29-31

He gives power to the weak and strength to the powerless. Even youths will become weak and tired, and young men will fall in exhaustion. But those who trust in the LORD will find new strength. They will soar high on wings like eagles. They will run and not grow weary. They will walk and not faint.

In this passage, Isaiah reminds us of the universal truth that every human has limited strength. But in contrast to people, God never grows tired. He has unlimited strength that he shares with those who trust him. To trust is to believe in the character and ability of another. Do you believe God is able to give you the strength you need to get through today? Proclaim your trust in him by claiming this promise for yourself.

Isaiah 46:3-4

I have cared for you since you were born. Yes, I carried you before you were born. I will be your God throughout your lifetime—until your hair is white with age. I made you, and I will care for you. I will carry you along and save you.

God's love for you began before you were born, and it will continue throughout your life, extending through eternity. How amazing to know that God doesn't stop caring for us for a single second of our lives! The next time you feel alone, abandoned, forgotten, or unimportant, meditate on these verses and the love your Creator has for you.

Proverbs 4:23

Guard your heart above all else, for it determines the course of your life.

Have you ever reacted to something that happened, only to find yourself surprised by the words that came out of your mouth or the intensity of your emotions? We often think that circumstances cause us to act in a certain way, but the truth is, circumstances trigger feelings that were already in our hearts. The book of Proverbs talks about the heart as the center of our thoughts and feelings. Every action and word flows from the heart; therefore it is important to be aware of what we let into it. When we fail to protect our hearts, we lose sensitivity to what is good and what is harmful. What would it look like to guard your heart? How can you be cautious about what you hear, see, watch, and choose to dwell on?

Isaiah 49:15-16

Can a mother forget her nursing child? Can she feel no love for the child she has borne? But even if that were possible, I would not forget you! See, I have written your name on the palms of my hands.

This is a beautiful verse for those who feel forgotten by God. His care for us is greater than a mother's care for her nursing child. A mother cannot forget her baby for even a moment because she is deeply bonded and intimately connected to her child. God feels the same about you. He loves you. He sees you. He cares for you even when you are unaware of it. You may not understand what he is doing in your life, but that doesn't mean he has abandoned you. Take these truths to heart and choose to believe that your heavenly Father will never forget you.

Isaiah 53:6

*All of us, like sheep, have strayed away.
We have left God's paths to follow our
own. Yet the L<small>ORD</small> laid on him
the sins of us all.*

Without the guidance and care of their shepherd, sheep wander away from the flock, leaving them vulnerable to danger. Isaiah says people behave the same way. If left to our own devices, we naturally stray from God our Shepherd and follow our own sinful desires, leading us down a dangerous path to destruction. But no matter how far we stray, God pursues us through his Son, Jesus. When Jesus died on the cross, he accepted the penalty for our sins so that we could follow God once again. Do you long to get on the right path? Pray for forgiveness, meditate on God's Word, and make choices that will lead you toward God. Your Shepherd will lovingly guide you back.

57

Isaiah 55:6

Seek the LORD while you can find him.
Call on him now while he is near.

Isaiah urged the people of Israel to seek God
while there was still time. God has invited all
of us into relationship with him and doesn't
want a single person to miss the opportunity
to know him personally. Seeking God means
looking for his presence and work in our
everyday lives, talking to him about everything, and listening for his voice as he leads
and guides. He is always offering us count-
less signs of his desire to be close to us. How
might God be trying to show you that he is
with you? Through beauty in nature? The
kindness of another? Unexplainable peace
in a desperate situation? An urge to choose
good over bad? Don't wait another day to look
for him. Call out to him while he is near.

Psalm 34:15

The eyes of the LORD watch over those who do right; his ears are open to their cries for help.

Every day presents us with many choices to do right or wrong. Most of the time these choices are subtle—exaggerating the truth, participating in gossip, being selfish rather than generous, or thinking about things we shouldn't. These choices are especially difficult when no one is near to hold us accountable. Psalm 34:15 reminds us that God sees each and every choice we make—both good and bad. When things get tough for those who try to do right, he promises to give them special care by listening to their pleas for help and reaching out to assist. Ask God to make you aware when you come to a crossroads of right versus wrong and to help you choose the path that is pleasing to him.

Jeremiah 1:5

I knew you before I formed you in your mother's womb. Before you were born I set you apart and appointed you as my prophet to the nations.

In this verse, God was calling Jeremiah to bring divinely inspired messages to people who were uninterested in hearing them. Imagine how difficult it would be to tell an entire nation that their downfall was a result of their own sin. But before God sent Jeremiah out with this message, he reminded him of his great care for him. Even though these words were spoken to Jeremiah, they are also the living Word of God, written down so they could be applicable to us as well. When God calls you to do hard things, first open his Word to receive encouragement. It will always give you the courage, perspective, and strength to accomplish what he has asked you to do.

Jeremiah 15:16

*When I discovered your words, I devoured them.
They are my joy and my heart's delight, for I
bear your name, O LORD God of Heaven's Armies.*

Jeremiah loved God's Word so much that
he *devoured* it. This is how God wants us
all to interact with his Word. The Bible
is described as the "eternal, living word
of God" (1 Peter 1:23) and is one of the
key ways he communicates to us today.
Therefore, it isn't meant to be merely
sampled. God wants us to devour and
consume its message. His words give joy
and purpose and life. As you meditate
on the passages in this book, remember
whose words you are reading. These verses
are the very words of your Creator, spoken
to you. Devour them and experience the
delight they bring to your heart.

Psalm 37:5

Commit everything you do to the LORD.
Trust him, and he will help you.

In this psalm, David contrasts the
godless with the faithful and names
many benefits of living in total
commitment to God. He concludes
that trusting God with all that we are
and have is not just our best hope
but also our greatest assurance. It
is not always easy to trust God in
a world where it seems like godless
people are getting ahead. But this
verse assures us that the almighty,
sovereign Creator of the universe will
help those who are dependent on his
leading. With God on your side, there
is no need to worry about what evil
people are doing.

Jeremiah 29:11-13

"I know the plans I have for you," says the LORD. "They are plans for good and not for disaster, to give you a future and a hope. In those days when you pray, I will listen. If you look for me wholeheartedly, you will find me."

King Nebuchadnezzar's army had captured God's people and brought them back to Babylon to live. Jeremiah wrote to tell the exiles that God had not abandoned or forgotten them. Even though they were in captivity because of their own foolishness, God reminded them that he had good plans for their future. He encouraged them to pray, because he would listen, and to look for him, because he would reveal himself. These verses reveal the faithfulness and graciousness of God's character. No matter how far from God you are or how bad your circumstances, God wants to give you a good future.

Jeremiah 31:3

I have loved you, my people, with an everlasting love. With unfailing love I have drawn you to myself.

What we believe about God impacts every part of our lives—our thoughts, attitudes, actions, and relationships. God spoke this beautiful verse to his people in exile, even though they had turned their backs on him time and again. He describes his love for them as *everlasting* and *unfailing*. How might your life look different if you truly internalized the love God has for you? Would you feel more secure and joyful? Would you be less burdened by guilt? Would you love others and yourself better because of the love you have received from God? Read this verse again, but this time put your name in place of "my people." Imagine God speaking this over you. Ask him to help you internalize his everlasting and unfailing love for you.

Lamentations 3:22-23

The faithful love of the LORD never ends!
His mercies never cease. Great is his faithfulness;
his mercies begin afresh each morning.

The book of Lamentations is a collection of poems that express deep sorrow over the ruin and devastation of Jerusalem after Babylon's army destroyed the city. The writer, who was likely the prophet Jeremiah, lamented over its loss, yet also expressed hope for its future. These verses offer encouragement for those who trust in the Lord, no matter how deep their sorrow or how great their adversity. *The faithful love of the Lord never ends! . . . His mercies begin afresh each morning.* Hold on to these verses during hard times. Their beautiful words offer a reason to wake up each day and to keep expecting good things for the future.

Proverbs 14:9

Fools make fun of guilt, but the godly acknowledge it and seek reconciliation.

Have you ever felt the uncomfortable twinge of conviction? Guilt can be either a burden or a gift. When we refuse to acknowledge guilt, our relationship with God is hindered. But admitting it helps us recognize that sin in our hearts causes damage to our souls and relationships. Only when we recognize our shortcomings can we work to defeat them and restore the damage done, making us right again with God and others. How do you respond when you feel guilt? Do you foolishly laugh it off, or do you explore it to determine whether it's pointing to something you need to deal with? Then do you acknowledge your sin before God and ask for his forgiveness? Choose to view your guilt as a gift that will lead you toward reconciliation.

Ezekiel 36:26-27

I will give you a new heart, and I will put a new spirit in you. I will take out your stony, stubborn heart and give you a tender, responsive heart. And I will put my Spirit in you so that you will follow my decrees.

God is passionate about holiness. Holiness doesn't happen by merely changing outward behavior; holiness happens through changed hearts. This isn't something people can do on their own but only as a result of God's supernatural help. When we realize that our sinful nature separates us from him, we can confess our sin to Jesus, receive his forgiveness, and commit to his way of living. Through the power of the Holy Spirit, he gives us a new heart, which frees us from captivity to sin. Then God sees us as holy! Has this happened in your life yet?

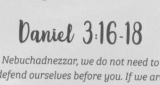

Daniel 3:16-18

*Nebuchadnezzar, we do not need to
defend ourselves before you. If we are
thrown into the blazing furnace, the God
whom we serve is able to save us. . . . But
even if he doesn't, we want to make it
clear to you . . . that we will never serve
your gods or worship the gold statue.*

King Nebuchadnezzar of Babylon
had built a statue and ordered
the people to worship it. When he
learned that three exiles from Judah
refused to obey, he sentenced them
to die in a blazing furnace. The most
compelling words in their response,
expressing unwavering faith in God's
ability to save them, are *But even if
he doesn't.* These men didn't doubt
God's power but were confident he
would be glorified, whatever the out-
come. The next time you ask God for
something, remind yourself also to
pray, "But whatever you decide, may
my actions bring you glory."

Psalm 37:23-24

The LORD directs the steps of the godly.
He delights in every detail of their lives.
Though they stumble, they will never fall,
for the LORD holds them by the hand.

These verses offer yet another benefit of a life committed to God: clear guidance and direction—not in a dictatorial kind of way but simply because he delights in every detail of our lives. Along with his guidance, he also gives us his support. He keeps us from falling and holds us by the hand as we walk through this life. We all long for God's direction, guidance, and support. Yet his Word tells us that as believers we already have these things! If you are in a season when life feels aimless, ask God to make his way visible to you. He is ready to provide wisdom and direction to all who ask.

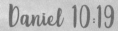

Daniel 10:19

Don't be afraid . . . for you are very precious to God.
Peace! Be encouraged! Be strong!

The prophet Daniel had a vision in which he was visited by an angel. Daniel was awestruck and unable to speak, but after the angel touched his lips, he opened his mouth and told the angel how weak and afraid he was. The angel touched and strengthened him, then spoke the words of this passage. They are the Lord's words to you, too. Whether God speaks to you through a vision, his Word, a friend, or the beauty of nature, he communicates to you from a place of love, always encouraging you. Imagine God speaking this message over you: *Do not be afraid. You are precious to me. Be encouraged. Be strong.* Meditate on these words to give you strength today.

Hosea 6:3

Oh, that we might know the LORD!
Let us press on to know him. He will respond to us
as surely as the arrival of dawn
or the coming of rains in early spring.

Sometimes we open our Bibles looking for encouragement, peace, hope, or a sense of God's nearness. These are not bad motives for reading Scripture, but if our expectations aren't met, we may feel disappointed. What if instead we opened God's Word with one motivation: to know him more? The prophet Hosea tells us that when we press on to know the Lord—through Scripture, prayer, or searching for his work and presence in our everyday lives—he will respond as surely as the sun comes up or the rain falls in the spring. As you read this devotional, don't just hope to experience good feelings; see it as an invitation to know your good God.

Amos 5:24

*I want to see a mighty flood of justice,
an endless river of righteous living.*

Prior to this verse, God had told his people he despised the hypocrisy of their religious gatherings, offerings, and songs. They were doing and saying all the "right" things but failing to live by them; in other words, failing to live justly and righteously. How often do we, too, worship God in church and then go about our days making decisions that are contrary to what God calls us to in his Word? Perhaps you're aware of hypocrisy in your own life. Or maybe you really do worship sincerely in church but struggle to make your actions reflect it during the week. Either way, each of us must learn to recognize the incongruencies between our faith and our actions, confess them to God, and rely on his help to close the gaps.

Psalm 40:8

I take joy in doing your will, my God,
for your instructions are written
on my heart.

What does it mean for God's instructions
to be written on our hearts? When we
read God's Word quickly, we just as quickly
tend to forget it. But if it is *written on our*
hearts, that means we can never forget it.
This happens only as we study, understand,
memorize, and practice what we read.
When we know God's Word and allow it to
shape the way we live, the result is deep joy
and a life with true meaning and purpose.
Do you take delight in reading the Bible?
Think about how you can be more serious
about meditating on God's Word so that it
becomes written on your heart.

Micah 6:8

O people, the LORD has told you what is good, and this is what he requires of you: to do what is right, to love mercy, and to walk humbly with your God.

This chapter in Micah describes a conversation between God and his people, Israel. In verse 6, Israel asks, "What can we bring to the LORD?" In other words, *What do you want from us?* The beautiful thing is that God didn't give them an ambiguous answer. He responded with *exactly* what he required of them (and us!): to do what is right, to love mercy, and to walk humbly with him. This is our God-given purpose. How can you do the right thing, both in your own life and for the sake of others? Who can you offer compassion and forgiveness to? How can you be faithful to walk with God throughout this day?

Zephaniah 3:17

The LORD . . . will take delight in you with gladness. With his love, he will calm all your fears. He will rejoice over you with joyful songs.

The book of Zephaniah is God's message that people will either be judged for their sin and pride or saved through repentance and humility. God takes sin seriously, but how wonderful that throughout the Bible he affirms his love for us and warns of the consequences of rebellion. This verse affirms the beautiful relationship he longs to have with anyone who wants to follow him. Think deeply about how much God loves you: He offers you eternal life through Jesus. He delights in how he made you. He can calm your fears with his love. And he can't help but sing joyful songs over you. Is anything holding you back from trusting God and receiving this kind of love?

Proverbs 15:1

A gentle answer deflects anger,
but harsh words make tempers flare.

Since Proverbs is a book about wise living, it includes an illustration describing how words impact our tempers. Of all the emotions we feel, anger is one of the most difficult to control. Anger itself is not wrong, but it becomes a problem when it leads us to sin against God and others. Thankfully, God in his wisdom has given us practical advice on how to handle anger—both our own and the anger of others. A gentle answer is always the wisest response. Sometimes we feel tempted to lash out with our words, but God's Word warns us this will only *make tempers flare*. How do you usually respond when you face anger? Ask God to help you remember this verse the next time you find yourself in a tense situation.

Zechariah 9:9

Shout in triumph, O people of Jerusalem! Look, your king is coming to you. He is righteous and victorious, yet he is humble, riding on a donkey— riding on a donkey's colt.

Zechariah had just warned foreign cities who were enemies of Judah about an upcoming invasion. But then he told the people of Jerusalem that their city would be protected by a king who was coming soon. This prophecy amazingly details an event that would occur more than five hundred years later: Jesus' entry into Jerusalem, when the people of Judah would acknowledge him as the long-awaited Messiah (Matthew 21:1-11). As you read the Bible and the story of salvation unfolds, watch for how God's promises are fulfilled and his humble character is manifested.

Malachi 3:10

Bring all the tithes into the storehouse so there will be enough food in my Temple. If you do, . . . I will open the windows of heaven for you. I will pour out a blessing so great you won't have enough room to take it in! Try it! Put me to the test!

God challenged his people to faithfully tithe, and in return, he promised to pour out his blessings. During this time, a tithe was a tenth of one's produce or livestock. God calls us to demonstrate this same faithfulness today with our income. We can always find an excuse to not give back to God a portion of what he has given to us; yet he challenges us to put him to the test. How might God be asking you to trust him to care for you as you more generously give to others?

Malachi 4:2

For you who fear my name, the Sun of Righteousness will rise with healing in his wings. And you will go free, leaping with joy like calves let out to pasture.

A theme of the book of Malachi is that the Day of the Lord is coming, when he will come in power and glory to save his people. This description of the Lord as the "Sun of Righteousness" is paralleled in the New Testament by Jesus' description of himself as the "light of the world" (John 8:12). Through his death and resurrection, Jesus offers eternal healing and joy for those who believe in and follow him. Take a minute to soak in the imagery here. What might it feel like to be fully healed, free, and leaping with joy? How does this verse give you hope for today as you think about your eternal future?

Psalm 42:1-2

As the deer longs for streams of water, so I long for you, O God. I thirst for God, the living God. When can I go and stand before him?

One of the beautiful things about the Psalms is that they give fresh language to help us as we pray. When you don't know what to pray, the Psalms are a great place to start. Slowly recite the verses above as a prayer to God. If the words don't resonate with you, ask God to give you a longing and a thirst for him. Reflect on what you use to try to quench your spiritual thirst instead of looking to him to meet this need. In what ways would you like to see the Lord satisfy your deepest desires for his presence in your life?

John 3:16

This is how God loved the world: He gave his one and only Son, so that everyone who believes in him will not perish but have eternal life.

Of all the verses in the Bible, John 3:16 may be the most well-known—perhaps because it sums up the Christian faith in one sentence. God loves *every single person* in the world. His love is displayed by sending his Son to die for our sins so we won't suffer the eternal consequences for them. Everyone who believes in Jesus will live eternally with God and also enjoy an abundant life on this side of heaven. Perhaps you have become so familiar with this verse that it has lost its impact. Read it again and dwell on the beautiful simplicity of the gospel message: *God loves you. Jesus died for your sins. If you believe this, you have life!*

John 1:12-13

To all who believed [Jesus] and accepted him, he gave the right to become children of God. They are reborn—not with a physical birth resulting from human passion or plan, but a birth that comes from God.

The beautiful thing about the Christian faith is its inclusivity, which doesn't discriminate based on who a person is, where they come from, or what they look like. Eternal salvation belongs to *all* who accept the truth that Jesus is God's Son and believe he died to take the punishment for their sins and was then resurrected. These verses also prompt an important question: *How would my life be different if I always acted on the truths that I'm accepted by God and he considers me his child?* Take a moment to ask God to help you internalize this passage so it impacts your thoughts, beliefs, and actions.

Psalm 42:5-6, 8

Why am I discouraged? Why is my heart so sad? I will put my hope in God! I will praise him again— my Savior and my God! . . . Each day the LORD pours his unfailing love upon me, and through each night I sing his songs, praying to God who gives me life.

One of the beautiful things about the Bible is that it often includes expressions of the raw emotions its writers were feeling, which readers can relate to. Everyone can recount a time when they felt discouraged and deeply sad. This psalm gives us an example of praying our emotions. The writer doesn't hold back from communicating his feelings to God. But he ends with praise, remembering God's unfailing love and care. What raw emotion is in your heart today? How can you express it to God and finish by praising him?

John 5:24

I tell you the truth, those who listen to my message and believe in God who sent me have eternal life. They will never be condemned for their sins, but they have already passed from death into life.

Jesus taught that eternal life doesn't begin once we die but the moment we choose to believe in him and accept his gift of salvation. You don't need to wait to experience a personal relationship with Jesus; you can have it right now. You can talk with him, grow with him, and be a part of his work on earth. Experiencing death will only lead to a glorious continuation of your relationship with him, lived out in his very presence. If you have chosen to love and follow Jesus, you are already experiencing eternal life!

Matthew 5:14-16

You are the light of the world. . . . No one lights a lamp and then puts it under a basket. Instead, a lamp is placed on a stand, where it gives light to everyone in the house. In the same way, let your good deeds shine out for all to see, so that everyone will praise your heavenly Father.

Jesus taught his disciples how to display the glory of God's Kingdom while living in the reality of a fallen world. Jesus calls all believers to light up the darkness by letting people see their good deeds. But as believers, it's not enough to just do good things; our good deeds should also reflect the character of our heavenly Father so that he gets the glory. Do your actions point others to God? How can you be a light in your neighborhood, workplace, and home?

Matthew 5:44-45

Love your enemies! Pray for those who persecute you! In that way, you will be acting as true children of your Father in heaven.

God's Word is often countercultural, compelling us toward actions that don't come naturally or easily. In these verses, Jesus taught the importance of loving our enemies. God calls us to love and pray for them instead of harboring hatred, bitterness, or resentment. When we do this, we reflect the heart of God to them. Jesus himself was betrayed, mocked, and even nailed to a cross, but he responded by loving and praying for those who opposed him. Perhaps someone in your life is hard to love or is actively working to make your life difficult. Start by praying for this person and asking God to help you see them as he does.

Proverbs 15:8-9

The LORD ... delights in the prayers of the upright. The LORD ... loves those who pursue godliness.

These verses underline the theme in Proverbs that the favor of God comes to those who are committed to pursuing a relationship with him. God loves and delights in those who strive to live in a way that pleases him. If we don't live with the intention of loving and serving God and others, then our prayers and our actions are empty—both to us and to God. Are you focused on living in a way that pleases your own desires? Or are you living to please your Creator? Think about the next task on your agenda and ask God to help you complete it in a way that brings him pleasure and glory.

Matthew 6:20-21

Store your treasures in heaven, where moths and rust cannot destroy, and thieves do not break in and steal. Wherever your treasure is, there the desires of your heart will also be.

The Bible refers to the center of thought and feeling as the "heart." Every action we take, emotion we feel, and word we speak flows from the heart. It's important to be aware of what our hearts truly treasure so that we can focus our time, attention, and energy on those things. How might God be calling you to store up treasure in heaven? Perhaps he wants you to give more generously, become involved in a local ministry, or invest in loving a specific group of people. Take time to think through what your heart really desires and ask God for a truly heavenly mind-set.

Matthew 6:25-26

That is why I tell you not to worry about every-day life—whether you have enough food and drink, or enough clothes to wear. Isn't life more than food, and your body more than clothing? Look at the birds. They don't plant or harvest or store food in barns, for your heavenly Father feeds them. And aren't you far more valuable to him than they are?

Worry is a natural part of life, but too much can distract and paralyze you. Worry becomes sinful when it prevents you from thinking about anything else, including God. The Bible teaches that we find rest from worry when we admit that we can't control the future and instead choose to entrust ourselves—and our loved ones—to the God who does. As you release your concerns to him, you'll find your troubles getting smaller and smaller, and you'll find yourself over-joyed rather than overwhelmed.

Matthew 6:33

*Seek the Kingdom of God above all else,
and live righteously, and he will give you
everything you need.*

Seeking God's Kingdom begins by acknowledging you are part of the bigger story
God is writing for the world. His plan is
that everyone would come to know him
and experience the joy that comes from
his forgiveness, presence, and promises of
eternal life. When you live with this Kingdom
perspective in mind, he gives you everything you need to play your role. God's view
of need is often much different from ours.
Jesus says not to worry about food, drink,
or clothing. These things are important, but
perhaps Jesus is suggesting that what we
truly need is to know God and do our part in
spreading his beautiful plan of redemption,
bringing him glory on earth.

Matthew 7:7-8

Keep on asking, and you will receive what you ask for. Keep on seeking, and you will find. Keep on knocking, and the door will be opened to you. For everyone who asks, receives. Everyone who seeks, finds. And to everyone who knocks, the door will be opened.

One of the most challenging tests the Lord may give is the opportunity to trust him through seasons of unanswered prayer. Jesus' words encourage us to pray with persistence and hope. The more we pray, the more our hearts become aligned with his and the more we understand his will for our lives. Perhaps God wants you to experience his love and faithfulness in new ways, or maybe he wants to open doors for you to discover how his desires really are best. When you pray, "Your will be done," God will lead you to a joyful and satisfying life.

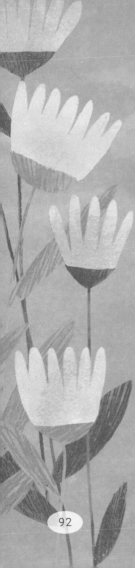

Matthew 7:24-27

Anyone who listens to my teaching and follows it is wise, like a person who builds a house on solid rock. Though the rain comes in torrents and the floodwaters rise . . . it won't collapse because it is built on bedrock. But anyone who hears my teaching and doesn't obey it is foolish, like a person who builds a house on sand. When the rains and floods come . . . , it will collapse with a mighty crash.

The analogies that Jesus uses here teach us about the foundation of the Christian faith. If we want to build our lives on something solid, then we must truly believe that Jesus is the Son of God and that his teachings will help us live with wisdom and purpose. Do you strive to know and follow Jesus by meditating on his words and obeying his message?

Matthew 8:25-26

The disciples went and woke him up, shouting, "Lord, save us! We're going to drown!" Jesus responded, "Why are you afraid? You have so little faith!" Then he got up and rebuked the wind and waves, and suddenly there was a great calm.

Picture a storm fierce enough to make grown men panic. Now imagine yourself in this scene, watching Jesus demonstrate complete control over nature. What might it be like to witness utter chaos dissolve into perfect calm? Now think about your own life. If Jesus is able to settle the wind and the waves, how much more is he able to settle the turmoil in your heart? Jesus never promised perfect circumstances, but this story affirms he can provide peace in the midst of them. Do you have faith he can do just that? What fears hold you back from trusting him?

Psalm 46:1

God is our refuge and strength,
always ready to help in times of trouble.

God promises that he is always ready to
help us when we need him. Yet often we look
for assistance from everyone else but him.
Asking others for help is good; the Bible urges
us to seek counsel from wise people. But we
should not do so to the neglect of seeking
counsel from God. When you find yourself
in trouble or faced with a big decision, who
initially comes to mind as the one who can
best help? From what source do you first seek
encouragement? This verse reminds us to go
directly to God. He is waiting for you to come
to him and is always ready to bestow comfort
and divine advice. He offers refuge and gives
strength to carry on. What do you need God's
help with today?

94

Matthew 10:32-33

Everyone who acknowledges me publicly here on earth, I will also acknowledge before my Father in heaven. But everyone who denies me here on earth, I will also deny before my Father in heaven.

These verses feel heavy and provoke accountability, don't they? Yet Jesus spoke them to his disciples to encourage them just before they went out to share about Jesus throughout their land. These words also apply to each of us who have chosen to follow Jesus. It's easy to sidestep conversations about our faith, but God calls us to "shout from the housetops for all to hear" (Matthew 10:27) the Good News that Jesus died for our sins. If this command from Jesus feels difficult, remind yourself of the reward—Jesus promises to acknowledge you before God for proclaiming your faith. It is worth the cost.

Matthew 10:42

If you give even a cup of cold water to one of the least of my followers, you will surely be rewarded.

So often Jesus' teachings are in opposition to the world's. Our culture teaches that the powerful, beautiful, wealthy, and successful should be held in high esteem. But Jesus calls his followers to a radically different way of life—to see and serve *the least*. Think about which of your coworkers and neighbors the world would consider to be the least. Ask God to open your spiritual eyes to see them and love them the way Jesus does. Remember, he promises to reward those who choose to obey.

Proverbs 16:18

Pride goes before destruction,
and haughtiness before a fall.

Pride has the power to destroy your life because it causes you to think you know more than God does. A person consumed by pride refuses to recognize they are completely dependent on their Creator. Pride is more than just arrogance; it is refusing to trust in God. This plays out through stubbornness, self-absorption, and a desire to control. Proverbs reminds us that wise living recognizes who God is and who we are in relation to him. Are there times when you doubt God's ability to lovingly lead you? Is it hard to believe he knows what is best for you in certain areas? Practice humility by asking God to show you the places where pride is hidden in your heart.

Matthew 11:28-30

Come to me, all of you who are weary and carry heavy burdens, and I will give you rest. Take my yoke upon you. Let me teach you, because I am humble and gentle at heart, and you will find rest for your souls. For my yoke is easy to bear, and the burden I give you is light.

Jesus extends a very simple invitation to everyone: "Come to me." He wants us to believe in him, to trust him, and to know him personally. And when we do, he promises to give rest to our weary souls. Perhaps you long for more specific information about how everything is going to work out in your life, but Jesus doesn't promise that. He simply offers to give you guidance and rest when you feel exhausted and overwhelmed. Come to him with your heart open to whatever he wants to teach you.

Matthew 14:27

Jesus spoke to them at once. "Don't be afraid," he said. "Take courage. I am here!"

Jesus had told his disciples to sail across the lake while he attended to the crowds they had just fed. While the disciples were crossing, a strong wind stirred up the waves. Jesus walked on the water to meet them, but they were afraid, thinking he was a ghost. Jesus called out, "Don't be afraid. . . . Take courage. I am here!" Sometimes Jesus quiets the storms and fears in our lives, and other times he meets us in the midst of them. Perhaps you have been caught in a storm for a while and are wondering if Jesus even sees your distress. Allow this verse to give you strength and encouragement as you wait for the storm to pass. You have nothing to fear because Jesus is with you.

Matthew 28:5-7

*The angel spoke to the women. "Don't be afraid!"
he said. "I know you are looking for Jesus, who was
crucified. He isn't here! He is risen from the dead,
just as he said would happen. Come, see where his
body was lying. And now, go quickly and tell his
disciples that he has risen from the dead."*

The Bible is more than just a compilation of
books to help us know God better; it's one
overarching beautiful story that reveals God's
plan to redeem his creation. And the entire
story has led up to this incredible moment,
when the angel announced, "He is risen from
the dead, just as he said would happen."
Ponder this pivotal time in history when
Jesus displayed his power over death and
confirmed he truly is the Son of God.

Psalm 46:10-11

"Be still, and know that I am God! I will be honored by every nation. I will be honored throughout the world." The LORD of Heaven's Armies is here among us.

Do you find yourself frantic and frazzled, constantly on the go as you strive to complete the next item on your to-do list? God is speaking these words to you in this very moment: *Be still, and know that I am God!* Being still may not come naturally. But it is only in quietness that you can absorb two important truths about God—that he is in control and that he is with you. So the next time fear or anxiety compels you to rush to another task, be still and remember who God is. Experiencing his power and presence will only enhance your productivity.

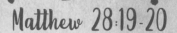

Matthew 28:19-20

Go and make disciples of all the nations, baptizing them in the name of the Father and the Son and the Holy Spirit. Teach these new disciples to obey all the commands I have given you. And be sure of this: I am with you always.

Before Jesus ascended into heaven, he gave his disciples a task: "Make disciples of all the nations." Jesus has commissioned us to do the same—to spread the Good News of his salvation and to train new believers in the faith. This can feel like an overwhelming task, but it doesn't have to be. Jesus began his ministry in one location, and you can do the same wherever God has placed you. Is God calling you to reach someone in your vicinity—your workplace, neighborhood, or home? Be encouraged by the promise that Jesus left his disciples with: "I am with you always."

Matthew 16:13-17

Jesus . . . asked his disciples, "Who do people say that the Son of Man is?" "Well," they replied, "some say John the Baptist, some say Elijah, and others say Jeremiah or one of the other prophets." Then he asked them, "But who do you say I am?" Simon Peter answered, "You are the Messiah, the Son of the living God." Jesus replied, "You are blessed, Simon son of John, because my Father in heaven has revealed this to you."

The disciples had spent much time with Jesus, and yet this is the first time Peter spoke of Jesus as the Messiah, the Son of God. Jesus called Peter blessed because God had revealed this great truth to him. Who is Jesus to you? Is he your safety net? Your obligatory master? Or is he your Savior and friend? Ask God to bless you by revealing who Jesus really is.

Psalm 56:8

You keep track of all my sorrows. You have collected all my tears in your bottle. You have recorded each one in your book.

This beautiful verse comes from a chapter in Psalms that describes David's choice to trust God to help him in the face of his enemies. We, too, can trust God in our hardships, because every part of us is precious to him—even the tears we cry. He not only sees those tears but also takes note of each and every one. Perhaps this is because he knows they represent the loss of something important to us. Since God goes to such great lengths to show us his care, he can be trusted to respond lovingly when we come to him with our grief and anguish.

Matthew 18:2-4

Jesus called a little child to him and put the child among them. Then he said, "I tell you the truth, unless you turn from your sins and become like little children, you will never get into the Kingdom of Heaven. So anyone who becomes as humble as this little child is the greatest in the Kingdom of Heaven."

Anyone who has raised children or spent much time with them wouldn't exactly describe them as humble. Children see themselves as the center of the universe, often demanding their own way. So when Jesus calls us to be as humble as little children, he is calling us to childlike trust and dependence. Young children naturally believe whatever their caregivers say and trust them to take care of their needs. God desires the same for you. How might he be calling you to come to him as a child today?

Matthew 18:21-22

Peter came to him and asked, "Lord, how often should I forgive someone who sins against me? Seven times?" "No, not seven times," Jesus replied, "but seventy times seven!"

Jesus taught his disciples about the generous forgiveness he desires from his followers. He calls us to forgive others seventy times seven; in other words, so often that we cannot keep track. True forgiveness means forgiving over and over again. If you are struggling to forgive someone today, remind yourself of the many times God has graciously forgiven you. How can you show the same kind of love and grace to this person who has wronged you?

Matthew 24:42, 44

So you, too, must keep watch! For you don't know what day your Lord is coming. . . . You also must be ready all the time, for the Son of Man will come when least expected.

Jesus told his disciples to keep watch and be ready for the day of his return. Because he didn't give specifics on when this day will happen, we, too, must always be ready. Don't put off God's Kingdom work until tomorrow. Right now, think about areas in your life where you might be procrastinating, putting off what you know God has called you to do. Perhaps inviting someone to church? Telling someone you love about Jesus? If you knew the Lord was coming tomorrow, how would you spend today stepping out in faith to do something God was asking of you?

Proverbs 17:9

Love prospers when a fault is forgiven, but dwelling on it separates close friends.

God, in his graciousness, has given us wisdom literature to instruct us on living well. And because much of life deals with relationships, Proverbs gives tidbits of wisdom for how to handle conflict with others. This particular verse contrasts a wise and foolish reaction to conflict. A wise person forgives, which inevitably allows love to flourish. But a foolish person dwells on another's faults and risks losing the friendship. Does this verse relate to any of your current relationships? Do you tend to be quick to forgive, or do you dwell on how others have hurt you? Forgiveness is not a feeling but a choice. Choose to stop dwelling on other's faults and to forgive instead.

Mark 2:14

Follow me and be my disciple.

Jesus spoke these words to Levi (also known as Matthew), a despised tax collector. Imagine everyone's shock when Jesus invited Levi to follow him and become one of his disciples. Jesus' invitation for relationship is for *everyone*, no matter what they have done or what their reputation is. Those who appear least deserving are the very ones Jesus seems to give special attention to. This verse encourages us not only to follow Jesus but also to follow his example of pursuing those who are in deep need of love and acceptance. What person in your life would Jesus give special attention to? How might the Holy Spirit be encouraging you to follow Jesus in this specific way?

Mark 8:34-37

If any of you wants to be my follower, you must give up your own way, take up your cross, and follow me. If you try to hang on to your life, you will lose it. But if you give up your life for my sake and for the sake of the Good News, you will save it. And what do you benefit if you gain the whole world but lose your own soul? Is anything worth more than your soul?

Living a self-centered life will never allow us to be devoted to Jesus. If we focus on the present world and our own desires, we won't inherit eternal life. But if we live to further God's work here on earth, he promises an eternal relationship with him that satisfies our deepest desires. What might God be calling you to give up in order to gain more of him?

Psalm 57:2

I cry out to God Most High, to God who will fulfill his purpose for me.

Most people long for a life of purpose and impact. And yet for so many, life feels empty and meaningless. This verse affirms the truth that God has a purpose for each person and is working to make it come to fruition for those who will let him. There may be seasons when life feels dull and aimless, but that doesn't mean God isn't at work. Choose to trust that he is opening doors to help you fulfill the purpose he has for you, even when you can't see or understand what is going on. Be alert to those doors opening. If you wake up every day intent on loving God and following him and watching for his lead, he promises that his plans and purpose for you *will* be fulfilled.

Mark 9:35

He sat down, called the twelve disciples over to him, and said, "Whoever wants to be first must take last place and be the servant of everyone else."

Jesus' words remind us that following him sometimes requires great sacrifice. He calls every believer to forfeit their own status and wants in order to care for and serve others. This calling isn't easy and doesn't always come naturally, especially when our sacrifices go unnoticed. But God is watching each time we love and serve those around us. Every time we sacrifice for another, our hearts reflect more of God's character. When you find yourself feeling resentful, bitter, or angry while serving others, ask the Holy Spirit to shape you into someone who is more loving, selfless, and generous.

Mark 10:31

Many who are the greatest now will be least important then, and those who seem least important now will be the greatest then.

Jesus spoke these words to his disciples after encountering a rich young man who wouldn't give up his possessions to follow Jesus. Jesus warned them how difficult it can be for the wealthy and those esteemed in the world's eyes to enter the Kingdom of God. Society's view of greatness is drastically different from God's. Throughout Jesus' life, we see him valuing the lowly, lonely, humble, poor, crippled, sick, and outcast. Whom do you view as "great"? Whom would God view as "great"? How might this verse shift your perspective and encourage you to value others differently?

Luke 6:31

Do to others as you would like them to do to you.

It's tempting to read this verse, which is also known as the Golden Rule, as "Be good to others, and they will be good to you." However, that isn't what Jesus is teaching here. A few verses later, he directs us to love our enemies and to lend without expecting anything in return. "Then your reward from heaven will be very great," Jesus says (verse 35). Have you recently done something for another with the hope that they would return the favor? If you find yourself disappointed or upset when someone doesn't respond to your efforts to care for them, it's a good indicator that you have misaligned motives. Is Jesus calling you to live out the Golden Rule with a specific person in your life?

Psalm 90:12, 14

Teach us to realize the brevity of life, so that we may grow in wisdom. . . . Satisfy us each morning with your unfailing love, so we may sing for joy to the end of our lives.

Remembering how short life really is can help us make wiser choices each day. If you woke up every morning remembering the brevity of life, you would probably be more present and loving to those around you. Maybe you wouldn't fret so much about the small stuff. Or perhaps you would make decisions with eternity in mind. As you begin each day, ask God to remind you of his unfailing love and to help you live wisely and joyfully since you don't know which day will be your last.

Luke 6:37-38

Do not judge others, and you will not be judged. . . . Forgive others, and you will be forgiven. Give, and you will receive. Your gift will return to you in full—pressed down, shaken together to make room for more, running over, and poured into your lap. The amount you give will determine the amount you get back.

It may seem as though Jesus is talking about two different things: judging others and generous giving. But these actions are actually linked to each other. Jesus calls us to generosity, especially in the area of forgiveness. Forgiving someone who has wronged you is good, but generous forgiveness—desiring good in the life of the one who wronged you—takes it a step further. Whichever you choose determines the amount of forgiveness you will receive. Whom might God be asking you to generously forgive?

Luke 24:32

They said to each other, "Didn't our hearts burn within us as he talked with us on the road and explained the Scriptures to us?"

Two of Jesus' followers were walking to a village called Emmaus, talking about all that had happened over the past three days—the death of Jesus and the reports of his resurrection. Then Jesus himself came up beside them and joined the conversation; yet these disciples didn't recognize him. He explained the Scriptures in a new way that touched their hearts, ministering to them through his presence and restoring their hope through his Word. How often do we fail to recognize Jesus ministering to us in our pain? Whatever your situation, keep your eyes open to the presence of Jesus and your heart open to receiving hope through his Word.

Proverbs 17:22

A cheerful heart is good medicine,
but a broken spirit saps a person's strength.

The mission of Satan, God's enemy and the enemy of our souls, is to kill, steal, and destroy everything good in our lives—especially our joy. But joy provides essential nourishment and healing for the heart; it can even transform our adversities into occasions of gratitude and celebration. Having a cheerful heart doesn't mean ignoring pain or sadness. It is choosing an attitude of appreciation and confident hope—despite our circumstances. What is one good gift you can thank God for today?

John 6:35

Jesus replied, "I am the bread of life. Whoever comes to me will never be hungry again. Whoever believes in me will never be thirsty."

Bread is a staple of life that satisfies our hunger and fills us up. By calling himself "the bread of life," Jesus is communicating his desire to give us spiritual satisfaction. Each of us has that deep longing to feel like our lives are full. Here Jesus is saying that only he can truly meet such a need—both now and for eternity. Are you currently experiencing spiritual hunger pangs? Do you long for authentic joy? Take Jesus' words to heart. Work to know him more and watch him fill your soul like nothing else can.

John 8:12

I am the light of the world. If you follow me, you won't have to walk in darkness, because you will have the light that leads to life.

Jesus called himself "the light of the world" because life without his presence is lived in darkness. Those who live in darkness can't see who they truly are and where they are going, and they can't see others for who they truly are either. Thus, they are unable to see what the point of life actually is. But when Jesus brings his light into our dark hearts, he helps us see so many things—the sin that displeases him, the Good News that transforms us, the divine beauty in the world, the best path to follow. With his light, you never again have to fumble around in this dark world. Are you living in darkness or living in the light of Jesus?

John 11:25-26

I am the resurrection and the life. Anyone who believes in me will live, even after dying. Everyone who lives in me and believes in me will never ever die. Do you believe this, Martha?

Mary and Martha were grieving the death of their brother, Lazarus. When Jesus came to see them after Lazarus had been in the tomb for four days, he comforted Martha with this hopeful message: Those who choose to trust Jesus will forever live in God's love and presence—even after death. Jesus continually reminds us to keep this eternal perspective while we live on this earth. Perhaps you, too, are in deep grief and need to hear Jesus speak these words over you. Cling to this promise from him. Hold tightly to the hope of salvation. Jesus will supply your peace, joy, courage, and security in times of sorrow.

Psalm 92:1-2

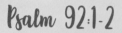

It is good to give thanks to the LORD,
to sing praises to the Most High.
It is good to proclaim your unfailing love
in the morning, your faithfulness in
the evening.

Psalm 92 is a beautiful hymn of
praise and thanksgiving to God.
It is good for our souls to worship
the Lord for his faithful love, from
the moment we open our eyes
at the beginning of a long day to
the moment we lay our heads back
down on the pillow. Wouldn't your
day be different if you began it by
praising God for his unfailing love
and ended it by thanking him for
the many ways he showed himself
faithful to you throughout the day?
You would certainly feel more secure,
content, and valued. Use this song
of praise to bookend your day with
worship to your Creator.

John 13:34-35

So now I am giving you a new commandment: Love each other. Just as I have loved you, you should love each other. Your love for one another will prove to the world that you are my disciples.

Jesus taught his disciples that they should be known for their love. He often quoted commandments from the Old Testament, including "Love the LORD your God with all your heart, all your soul, and all your strength" (Deuteronomy 6:5) and "Love your neighbor as yourself" (Leviticus 19:18). Jesus took these commandments one step further when he said we are to love others as he does. Throughout his life, Jesus modeled radical love by loving the morally corrupt and socially outcast, friends who had betrayed and abandoned him, and those who persecuted and crucified him. This kind of love will stand out in the world and prove that we are his disciples.

John 14:2-3

There is more than enough room in my Father's home. If this were not so, would I have told you that I am going to prepare a place for you? When everything is ready, I will come and get you, so that you will always be with me where I am.

When Jesus talks about his "Father's home," he is referring to heaven. Not only is there plenty of room for you in heaven; Jesus has also *specially* prepared a place for you there. Imagine what it might feel like to arrive in paradise with your new home all ready for you—and realize it's even better than you imagined! This isn't a matter of housekeepers preparing your space; Jesus himself is getting everything ready, just for you. Then he will come for you, and you'll live with him forever. Does this imagery have a positive impact on your view of heaven?

Psalm 95:6-7

Come, let us worship and bow down. Let us kneel before the LORD our maker, for he is our God. We are the people he watches over, the flock under his care. If only you would listen to his voice today!

Have you ever thought of taking prayer a step further by positioning your body in a posture of humility? This psalm invites us to engage in worship through the physical response of bowing and kneeling before the Lord. Bowing and kneeling signify that our hearts have an attitude of meekness and submission toward the one who always watches over us and keeps us under his care. Take a few minutes to kneel or bow before the Lord your Maker, thanking him for who he is and asking him to open your heart to him.

John 14:6

I am the way, the truth, and the life. No one can come to the Father except through me.

Our culture doesn't like to be told there is only one way to do something, so Jesus' claim to be the *only* way to God may seem narrow. However, it is quite the opposite: God offers salvation to *all* who believe in his Son, Jesus. In his grace, God has given us a clear way to know him, and that is through the life, death, and resurrection of Jesus Christ. You don't have to guess at how you can have eternal life. You don't have to earn your way. You simply need to accept that Jesus is the only way to heaven and follow him by faith. No one is excluded from the opportunity to respond to his invitation. Thank God for making the way to salvation clear and accessible.

John 15:5

Yes, I am the vine; you are the branches.
Those who remain in me, and I in them,
will produce much fruit. For apart from me
you can do nothing.

This verse paints yet another beautiful picture of the Christian life. Without a connection to the main trunk, a vine's branches cannot sustain themselves. They will become lifeless. It's the same for us in our relationship with Christ: To produce spiritual fruit—to grow in character and become more *like* Christ—we must be connected to him. Just as the vine nourishes the branch, our faith is nourished through life-giving fellowship with God. We cannot grow when we live apart from Christ. What is one specific way you can remain connected to him as you go about your day?

John 17:15-18

I'm not asking you to take them out of the world, but to keep them safe from the evil one. They do not belong to this world any more than I do. Make them holy by your truth; teach them your word, which is truth. Just as you sent me into the world, I am sending them into the world.

Jesus' final prayer with his disciples served to remind them that those who trust in him do not belong to this world. They have a heavenly perspective that leads them to love God and others. There is nothing Satan would like more than to prevent us from doing this. How does Satan lure your focus away from eternity and onto the things of the world? Ask God to protect you from evil so you can live a holy life, spreading the Good News of his love and truth.

Proverbs 19:20

Get all the advice and instruction you can, so you will be wise the rest of your life.

God's Word emphasizes the importance of living in community. This verse reminds us that no one is wise enough to grasp all the issues related to a problem nor to anticipate all the possibilities for solving it. We need the advice and instruction of others in order to make wise decisions. In what areas do you struggle with asking for advice? When do you find yourself resisting instruction? Ask God to help you let go of your pride so you can be open to receiving godly counsel. God may use the voice of a trusted friend to speak an important truth into your life.

Acts 1:11

"Men of Galilee," they said, "why are you standing here staring into heaven? Jesus has been taken from you into heaven, but someday he will return from heaven in the same way you saw him go!"

The book of Acts begins with Jesus' ascension into heaven, which took place after he had commissioned his disciples to take the Good News of his death and resurrection to the world. While the disciples were watching, Jesus was taken up into a cloud, "and they could no longer see him" (verse 9). Two angels appeared to tell the disciples that Jesus had been taken away but would return again. Jesus not only promised to send the Holy Spirit but also sent angels to reassure them of his return. Jesus *will* come back again. How might this truth change the way you approach today?

Romans 1:16

I am not ashamed of this Good News about Christ. It is the power of God at work, saving everyone who believes.

Before the apostle Paul's conversion, he was known for his brutal persecution of Christians. When he experienced the power of God in his life, he couldn't help but carry out his mission to shamelessly preach the truth about Jesus to everyone. Have you ever struggled with feeling ashamed of sharing your faith? Perhaps you don't want to experience embarrassment, isolation, or ridicule for believing in Jesus. Yet if God has changed your heart, answered specific prayers, or blessed you with other miracles in your life, it's impossible to stay silent. Tell someone your story, and don't be ashamed to share the Good News with them.

Psalm 103:11-12

His unfailing love toward those who fear him is as great as the height of the heavens above the earth. He has removed our sins as far from us as the east is from the west.

How could God even begin to describe the depth of his love for us? The Bible often uses imagery to create a visual picture in our minds. Imagine the height of the heavens or the span from east to west. It has no end, and neither does God's love for you. Nothing you do could ever make him love you any less. What is keeping you from *truly* believing this? How would your life be different if you put this truth into action? Reflect on these great words describing God's love and fully embrace his unconditional love and forgiveness for you.

Romans 3:22

We are made right with God by placing our faith in Jesus Christ. And this is true for everyone who believes, no matter who we are.

When Paul wrote the book of Romans, there was major tension in the church between the Jews and the Gentiles—those from the nations. The Jews were God's chosen people and treated the Gentiles as spiritually unworthy. However, one of Paul's missions was to bring the message of salvation to all people and unite both groups through their faith in Jesus. The theme of exclusivity still exists in the church today. Some people are not welcomed based on their appearance, race, or socioeconomic status. Do these tensions exist within your church? How about within your own heart? Think about Paul's words—we are *all* reconciled to God when we place our faith in Jesus Christ.

Romans 3:23-25

Everyone has sinned; we all fall short of God's glorious standard. Yet God, in his grace, freely makes us right in his sight. He did this through Christ Jesus when he freed us from the penalty for our sins. For God presented Jesus as the sacrifice for sin. People are made right with God when they believe that Jesus sacrificed his life, shedding his blood.

The foundation of the Christian faith is beautifully summed up in this passage from Romans. It reminds us of our spiritual neediness and how God has made it possible to be right with him through the sacrifice of his Son, Jesus. Are you in a season where you've lost sight of these truths? Have you become overly focused on things that are irrelevant to your faith? Use these verses to anchor your thoughts in the knowledge that God loves you and that through Jesus, your sins are forgiven.

Romans 5:1-2

Since we have been made right in God's sight by faith, we have peace with God because of what Jesus Christ our Lord has done for us. Because of our faith, Christ has brought us into this place of undeserved privilege where we now stand, and we confidently and joyfully look forward to sharing God's glory.

Hope is a powerful thing. When it is lost, we fall into depression and despair. These verses assure us of the hope we have in the saving power of Jesus Christ. Because of our faith in him, God promises we will be filled with peace and joy unlike anything we have ever experienced—both now and for all eternity. What situation, relationship, or task feels hopeless today? Ask Jesus for his perspective and trust him to provide the peace and joy—and hope—that he promises.

Psalm 118:5-7

In my distress I prayed to the LORD, and the LORD answered me and set me free. The LORD is for me, so I will have no fear. What can mere people do to me? Yes, the LORD is for me; he will help me.

Have you ever known someone who was completely *for* you—someone who was always available to offer support and had your best interests at heart? This is how God loves you! He is rooting for you, encouraging you to become all he created you to be. When you pray, he answers by giving what is best for you. When you long for companionship, he is right there. When you need support, he encourages you. Develop the spiritual skill of noticing him and hearing his voice. If the God of the universe cares this much about you, what do you really have to fear today?

Romans 5:3-5

We can rejoice, too, when we run into problems and trials, for we know that they help us develop endurance. And endurance develops strength of character, and character strengthens our confident hope of salvation. And this hope will not lead to disappointment. For we know how dearly God loves us, because he has given us the Holy Spirit to fill our hearts with his love.

Suffering changes us for better or worse. Some dwell on the past and lose hope for the future, becoming isolated and bitter. As believers, we are called to view our trials differently. Paul says we can rejoice because we know God is strengthening not only our character but also our hope in the promise of salvation. If you are in a painful season, lean into God, not away from him. Read his Word daily and remind yourself of his presence and promises.

Romans 5:8

God showed his great love for us by sending Christ to die for us while we were still sinners.

In our culture, we pay honor and respect to those who die trying to save others—especially when the people they rescue are respectable or morally good. The amazing thing about Christ is that he didn't die for those who are good. He died for those who are *still sinners*, proving how much he loves us. This beautiful verse supports a particular theme woven throughout Romans: We can't *do* anything to earn salvation—it's a free gift that everyone can access through faith in Christ. The next time you find yourself trying to earn God's favor, remember that if you have given your life to Jesus, you already have his approval. What could be better news than this?

Proverbs 21:26

*Some people are always greedy for more,
but the godly love to give!*

While our culture encourages us to make more money and spend it on ourselves, the Bible focuses on how we should give generously to others. Followers of Jesus love to give because they recognize that everything they have is from his hands. For them, generosity is a joyful opportunity to share God's blessings. Giving financially is just one way of sharing. You can also be generous with your time, talents, resources, and even your home. Perhaps generosity is an area of difficulty for you. If so, think about these questions: How has God blessed you? How might he want to multiply that blessing if you were to give generously out of what he has given you? Then ask the Lord for faith to become a person who loves to give. You won't regret it!

Romans 6:23

The wages of sin is death,
but the free gift of God is eternal life
through Christ Jesus our Lord.

Romans 6:23 is an often-quoted verse that emphasizes the *Good* in *Good News*. A wage is payment for work we have done, while a gift is the opposite—it is given without expectation of anything in return. Paul emphasizes that because Jesus Christ died to pay the penalty for our sins, we who place our trust in him are justified before God. As a result, we are no longer subject to the law of sin and eternal death. Have you grasped the significance of this crucial truth? We've done nothing to earn God's amazing gift, yet because of his great love for us, he has freely given it. Take a moment to thank God that his grace isn't based on your efforts.

Romans 8:26

The Holy Spirit helps us in our weakness. For example, we don't know what God wants us to pray for. But the Holy Spirit prays for us with groanings that cannot be expressed in words.

Do you ever feel like you have no words to pray? Pain, confusion, exhaustion, grief, anxiety, and emptiness can hinder your expression to God in prayer. When we don't know what to pray, the Holy Spirit intercedes and prays for us. His prayers for us aren't hollow—he prays with *groanings* that we cannot begin to understand. The next time you sit in silence before God, longing to pray but unable to find the words, remind yourself of the one who is already praying on your behalf.

Romans 8:28

We know that God causes everything to work to-gether for the good of those who love God and are called according to his purpose for them.

Sometimes in life we go through difficult, painful circumstances that also seem utterly meaningless. We can't imagine our suffering will accomplish anything. *What a sad waste of my time, energy, and emotion*, we lament. It's during these times that we need to cling to this beautiful promise in Scripture: God turns everything into good—even the evil, gut-wrenching agonies of life. From begin-ning to end, we read stories in the Bible that show God keeping his promise to turn bad into good. Perhaps you're in the trenches of deep sadness and have yet to see God carry out this promise. Cling to this verse. Instead of believing your pain is meaningless, choose to trust that God will work everything together for your benefit.

Psalm 118:24

This is the day the LORD has made.
We will rejoice and be glad in it.

Every day is a gift granted to us by our Creator. Because God wastes nothing, he doesn't create worthless days. God has given you the gift of life for another day, and he has a purpose for you in it. How might your day unfold differently if you woke up every morning with this verse on your mind? Would you feel more grateful or choose an attitude of joy instead of despair, resentment, or bitterness? Would you be more alert to God's presence and activity and in turn more present to those around you? Try reciting this verse first thing in the morning for the next week and watch what happens to your attitude and awareness of God's presence.

Romans 8:38-39

Nothing can ever separate us from God's love. Neither death nor life, neither angels nor demons, neither our fears for today nor our worries about tomorrow—not even the powers of hell can separate us from God's love. No power in the sky above or in the earth below—indeed, nothing in all creation will ever be able to separate us from the love of God that is revealed in Christ Jesus our Lord.

What can separate us from Christ's love? Paul answers this question in verse 38: *nothing.* Absolutely nothing can ever separate us from the love of Jesus. Knowing this, do you really have anything to fear? Do you need to worry about what others think of you? Do you need to live in guilt and shame? Embracing this truth will change the way you see yourself and the way you live.

1 Corinthians 10:12-13

If you think you are standing strong, be careful not to fall. The temptations in your life are no different from what others experience. And God is faithful. He will not allow the temptation to be more than you can stand. When you are tempted, he will show you a way out so that you can endure.

Each of us has a particular area of weakness where the tempter strikes. Do you know where you are most vulnerable? Being "careful not to fall" means being aware of what tempts you and alert to the triggers that might cause you to sin. If you fail to even notice you're being tempted, you will also fail to see God's escape plan. How might Satan be tempting you right now? Ask God to help you grow in awareness so you can draw on his power to stand strong.

Psalm 119:11

I have hidden your word in my heart,
that I might not sin against you.

What does it mean to hide God's Word in our hearts? Just as we tuck good memories away to ponder later, Scripture can be memorized to recall as needed. As we read, memorize, and meditate on God's Word, its divine power is absorbed into our souls, changing our thoughts, feelings, and actions to become more like Christ's. It's great to have the Bible easily accessible on our phones, but it's more important to have Scripture in our hearts. The passages we commit to memory will always be with us and will come to mind when we need them most. What verse would you like to commit to memory this week so that its message can live in your heart?

1 Corinthians 12:4, 7, 27

There are different kinds of spiritual gifts, but the same Spirit is the source of them all.... A spiritual gift is given to each of us so we can help each other.... All of you together are Christ's body, and each of you is a part of it.

Have you ever felt like you have nothing special to offer the world? This passage reminds us of an important truth: *Every* believer is given at least one unique spiritual gift by the Holy Spirit to help advance God's Kingdom. Therefore, it is important to know what yours is. If you aren't sure, start by asking God and trustworthy friends. Then ask yourself this question: *What am I good at?* Spiritual-gifts assessments can help as well. The more you use your gift to help others, the greater your impact for God's work.

147

1 Corinthians 15:58

Be strong and immovable. Always work enthusiastically for the Lord, for you know that nothing you do for the Lord is ever useless.

Nothing is more defeating than feeling like our hard work is useless, unappreciated, or wasted. This verse gives us hope—a reason to work enthusiastically at whatever job God has set before us. In Romans, Paul focuses on salvation through faith in Jesus, and in 1 Corinthians, he offers practical application for what that means for our work. Jesus' resurrection claimed victory over death, both for himself and for us. Death isn't the end of our stories if we follow him. When we fully embrace this truth, it lends perspective to our work and daily lives. Whatever you do, work hard in the name of Jesus, remembering that everything you do for him is an investment in your eternal life. It will not be wasted!

2 Corinthians 5:17

Anyone who belongs to Christ has become a new person. The old life is gone; a new life has begun!

Have you ever dreamed of a fresh start—an opportunity for a new beginning to wipe the slate clean? No matter what has happened in your past or what sins you presently struggle with, it's never too late to start over. Those who ask Jesus to be their Savior become new people on the inside because God sends his Spirit to reside in their hearts. Even if you have been a believer for a long time and still feel like you need a fresh start, God promises to continually bring new life to your heart if you allow him. Thank him for being a Father who delights in second chances and new beginnings.

Proverbs 24:13-14

Honeycomb is sweet to the taste.
In the same way, wisdom is sweet to your soul.
If you find it, you will have a bright future,
and your hopes will not be cut short.

Do you crave wisdom as much as you crave your favorite dessert? Do you long to know how to best manage your relationships, emotions, money, and time? This proverb promises that divine wisdom will result in the health of our souls, because we are fully confident in God's purposes for our lives. This leads us to make better choices every day. What are you dealing with right now that could use a good dose of the Lord's wisdom? Search his Word, pray for his insight, and ask godly people to help you. Then make your decision with the assurance that no matter what happens, your future with God is secure.

Galatians 5:22-23

The Holy Spirit produces this kind of fruit in our lives: love, joy, peace, patience, kindness, goodness, faithfulness, gentleness, and self-control.

How do you know if you are growing in your faith and "producing fruit"? Go through the list of fruits in these verses and ask yourself if these character traits are ripening in your life. Are you growing in your love for God and others, especially those whom you dislike? Are you making progress in developing patience with people who annoy you? Are your words more kind today than yesterday? Have you done better at telling the whole truth? Take a moment and think about which of these fruits still need to grow. Ask the Holy Spirit for awareness in this area to help you become more like Christ.

Ephesians 1:4

Even before he made the world, God loved us and chose us in Christ to be holy and without fault in his eyes.

Before God created the world, he had *you* in mind. He knew exactly when you would be born and for what purpose. Just as expectant parents are bursting with anticipation as they await the arrival of their child, God has greatly anticipated your existence since the beginning of time. Therefore, your life has great meaning. At the same moment you ask Jesus to forgive your sins and commit your life to him, God views you as *holy*, as though you had never sinned. He sees you as you'll be when you're reigning with him in his eternal, heavenly Kingdom: free from any fault or imperfection. Does this fill you with hope for your future?

Psalm 119:18

Open my eyes to see the wonderful truths in your instructions.

This verse would be an excellent prayer to pray every time you open God's Word. When we come to him with willing and humble hearts, God promises to reveal divine wisdom, insight, knowledge, and truth—often tailor-made to our specific circumstances. It helps us know him better and live out our faith more effectively. This prayer puts our hearts in a posture of humility so we're prepared to receive the supernatural help and wisdom that God's Word offers. It also reminds us of our utter dependence on our Creator. When was the last time you took a moment to pray for insight before you opened your Bible? Expect God's wonderful truths to produce great change within your heart.

Ephesians 2:10

We are God's masterpiece. He has created us anew in Christ Jesus, so we can do the good things he planned for us long ago.

Just as a beautiful mosaic is made from many pieces, God forms a masterpiece with the messy, broken, and dirty pieces of your past. God wants to recreate you to bring glory to his name and to give you the wonderful future he planned for you since the beginning. Trust that as time passes, he will exchange the ashes of your life for "a crown of beauty" (Isaiah 61:3)—a beauty that you never thought possible.

Ephesians 3:12

Because of Christ and our faith in him, we can now come boldly and confidently into God's presence.

Only a few people have unlimited access to the president of the United States. As powerful as the president is, our God, as the creator and sustainer of the universe, has ultimate power over everything—what is seen and unseen. Because of our faith in Jesus, we have full, unlimited access to this mighty God. We can come *boldly* and *confidently* into his presence, not with fear or cowardice. He actually wants us to draw near to him. The next time you pray, think about who you are praying to. Thank him for being the one and only God who can hold the universe together and still be available to converse with you.

Ephesians 5:15-17

Be careful how you live. Don't live like fools, but like those who are wise. Make the most of every opportunity in these evil days. Don't act thoughtlessly, but understand what the Lord wants you to do.

Every day is filled with choices to do things that matter or things that don't. With so many distractions and temptations, it's a challenge to live wisely, making the most of every opportunity that comes our way. When we carve out time to commune with God, prayerfully read his Word, and listen to his voice, his direction becomes more clear. We develop spiritual vision, which helps us see what is most important and what we should let go of. The more we allow God's Word and Spirit to fill our thoughts, the less thoughtless our actions will be. How can you be intentional about spending time with God today?

Psalm 119:97-98

Oh, how I love your instructions! I think about them all day long. Your commands make me wiser than my enemies, for they are my constant guide.

Do you really believe the Bible can guide you better than any other source? How often do you open it to receive God's wisdom? This passage doesn't suggest that God's instructions are intended to guide us periodically—it says his commands are our "constant guide," supplying us with divine understanding that those opposed to God cannot access. Since his Word is the wisest guidance we could ever receive, we'll want to refer to it often and know it well. When you face circumstances you don't know how to handle, where do you go first? The internet? Your family and friends? The next time you need advice, prayerfully open God's Word and watch him give you exactly what you need for that moment.

Ephesians 6:7

Work with enthusiasm, as though you were working for the Lord rather than for people.

When we work to gain the appreciation or validation of others, we will almost always be left feeling disappointed. No one can fully understand the effort and care that goes into our work, especially when much of it goes unseen. But God sees what we do, and he encourages us to work with enthusiasm—as though we were working for him instead of others. Imagine God beside you as you work today. Think of yourself as working *for* him, and remind yourself that when you partner with the Lord, you are building his Kingdom on earth! This will help you work with a joyful and thankful heart, remembering that nothing you do for God is ever wasted.

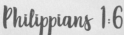

Philippians 1:6

I am certain that God, who began the good work within you, will continue his work until it is finally finished on the day when Christ Jesus returns.

Paul was confident that God would help the Philippian believers progress spiritually. With this "good work" would come an attitude that would bless others. Paul later describes this attitude as "the desire and the power to do what pleases [God]" (2:13). Our part is to "work hard to show the results of [our] salvation" (2:12). God wants us to be active in our faith, not passively waiting for him to work through us. He wants us to participate in what he is doing—through praying, studying his Word, attending to his presence, and serving others. How might God be asking you to act on his good work in and through you today?

159

Proverbs 27:17

As iron sharpens iron, so a friend sharpens a friend.

The Bible gives wise instruction on the topic of friendship because God knows how important it is to walk through life with a good friend by our side. God's Word describes a good friend as someone who is loving, loyal, generous, sympathetic, and always ready to offer grace. However, it also mentions the importance of friends who will gently confront and challenge each other—a not-so-pleasant task. An important question to ask yourself before you "sharpen" another is, *Am I challenging this person because I want them to become more like Christ or because what they are doing is bothering me?* To be on the receiving end of the sharpening is also difficult. Pray that God would open your heart to receive loving critique in order to refine your character and help you become more like Jesus.

Philippians 3:13-14

I focus on this one thing: Forgetting the past and looking forward to what lies ahead, I press on to reach the end of the race and receive the heavenly prize for which God, through Christ Jesus, is calling us.

When running a race, athletes must always keep the end goal in mind—crossing the finish line. When the going gets tough, they picture the final reward, even if it's just the satisfaction of finishing. Keeping this in mind motivates them to work hard in the present moment. Paul encourages us to do the same as we run our "spiritual" race. We visualize our end goal—eternal life with God in a perfect world—so we can live our present moments with purpose. What goals keep you motivated? Finishing a degree? Buying a house? Retirement? How might shifting your goal to enjoying eternal heavenly rewards change how you live today?

Philippians 4:4, 6-7

I say it again—rejoice! . . . Don't worry about anything; instead, pray about everything. Tell God what you need, and thank him for all he has done. Then you will experience God's peace, which exceeds anything we can understand. His peace will guard your hearts and minds.

Worry lives in the future, fretting over something that might never happen. Rejoicing over what is good in your life will keep you in the present. When you "pray about everything," start by praising God for what is good in your life. Then go ahead and tell him about your concerns. Whenever worry invades your mind, use it as a reminder to pray in the present. This is the way to guard your heart and mind from spiraling into anxiety. It helps you experience God's peace immediately. What specific worry can you transform into prayer today?

Philippians 4:8

Fix your thoughts on what is true,
and honorable, and right, and pure, and lovely,
and admirable. Think about things that are
excellent and worthy of praise.

Our thoughts hold great power over us because they impact our emotions and influence our actions. When we allow our minds to rabbit-trail down paths of unhealthy and sinful thoughts, we suddenly find ourselves far away from the kinds of attitudes God desires for us. But if we fix our thoughts on God, we will experience peace—and peace brings joy, contentment, and satisfaction. Over time, with awareness and practice, our thoughts will naturally bend toward godliness instead of selfishness, which will transform us from the inside out. What habits keep your mind focused on the darker side of life? How might you shift your gaze to whatever is "excellent and worthy of praise"?

163

Psalm 119:105

Your word is a lamp to guide my feet and a light for my path.

Though the Bible was written by godly people thousands of years ago, it is still the inspired and living Word of God that helps people live godly lives today. How amazing that the God of the universe would actually want to help us navigate through every stage of life! No matter what season we are in, he has something to say to us. Reading his Word keeps us in the presence of the one who created us for a purpose, knows us best, and can guide us along the best pathway for our lives. Where do you need guidance today? Ask the Lord to shine his light on your journey.

Philippians 4:12-13

I have learned the secret of living in every situation, whether it is with a full stomach or empty, with plenty or little. For I can do everything through Christ, who gives me strength.

Paul had seen it all. He had eaten at great feasts but had also almost starved to death. He had been treated with great respect as well as beaten to the edge of death. Along the way he found the secret to being content no matter what his circumstances were. He saw each occasion as a divine opportunity to rely on Christ's power to help him and to talk about his Lord in hopes of bringing others to faith. In this way he could enter any situation with the anticipation that God would work good through it. How might your day be different if you approach every event in this same way?

1 Timothy 6:6-7

True godliness with contentment is itself great wealth. After all, we brought nothing with us when we came into the world, and we can't take anything with us when we leave it.

The contentment that Paul experienced and encouraged us to attain is among life's most elusive qualities. The answer to the question "How much is enough?" always seems to be "Just a little bit more." So how can we resist the urge to find contentment in the pursuit of happiness, pleasure, or material possessions? True contentment is found in knowing what brings lasting gratification. When we follow Jesus, we know that this world is not all there is. We have an eternal relationship with our Creator, who satisfies our deepest longings. The "stuff" of this world doesn't matter anymore for those who keep this perspective. Ask God to help you trust that he is enough.

Psalm 121:1-2

I look up to the mountains—does my help come from there? My help comes from the LORD, who made heaven and earth!

This psalm was written for those on a pilgrimage to worship the Lord in Jerusalem. Whether you are looking to the hills of Jerusalem or simply to the hills ahead, ask yourself, *Where does my help come from?* Perhaps you have a long journey before you. Maybe you feel overwhelmed and afraid to scale the difficult hills in your life. Or perhaps you see the destination but need help getting there. Read this beautiful verse again and say, "My help comes from the LORD, who made heaven and earth!" You can have confidence in the journey ahead because the Lord is your expert guide.

2 Timothy 4:7-8

I have fought the good fight, I have finished the race, and I have remained faithful. And now the prize awaits me—the crown of righteousness. . . . And the prize is not just for me but for all who eagerly look forward to his appearing.

Don't we all want to be able to say these words when we reach the end of our lives? *I have fought the good fight, finished the race well, and remained faithful through it all.* If this is the way we want to conclude our stories, then we must begin living this way now. Are you spreading the Good News to a broken world? Are you living with your eye on eternity? Are you faithful in both the big and small things? If so, this passage promises the best prize at the end of your race—the crown of righteousness.

Hebrews 12:1-2

Since we are surrounded by such a huge crowd of witnesses to the life of faith, let us strip off every weight that slows us down, especially the sin that so easily trips us up. And let us run with endurance the race God has set before us. We do this by keeping our eyes on Jesus, the champion who initiates and perfects our faith.

Great faith can be defined as unwavering trust in God's promises. Right before this passage, the writer of Hebrews gives many examples of people from the Old Testament who displayed great faith. Here he describes them as watching us from heaven as we run our own race of faith. So how can *you* faithfully endure to the end? The answer is in these five words: *Keep your eyes on Jesus.* He will help and encourage you until you cross the finish line and reach perfection.

Hebrews 13:1-2

Keep on loving each other as brothers and sisters. Don't forget to show hospitality to strangers, for some who have done this have entertained angels without realizing it!

Hospitality is an important part of loving others. These verses encourage us to show hospitality not only to those we love but also to those we may not even know. There are plenty of reasons we avoid hosting others—busy schedules, messy homes, feelings of inadequacy. But beautiful decor and gourmet meals have little to do with hospitality. Hospitality is about cultivating a safe space for others to experience the welcoming presence of God. Don't be distracted with making the perfect meal or having a spotless house. Just be generous with what you have, set aside your insecurities, and enjoy the people who come into your home. It is your presence, not your presentation, that makes others feel welcome.

Proverbs 31:8-9

Speak up for those who cannot speak for themselves; ensure justice for those being crushed. Yes, speak up for the poor and helpless, and see that they get justice.

We are all concerned with our own protection, but God has also given us the responsibility of protecting others. Being a follower of Jesus requires more than knowing what is good; it demands *doing* good. Someday God will set the whole world right. But for now, he wants you to partner with him to bring justice for those who cannot speak up for themselves—the crushed, the poor, and the helpless. What injustices break your heart? Pray that God would stir you to action to support those who desperately need it.

James 5:16

The earnest prayer of a righteous person has great power and produces wonderful results.

One of the most challenging tests the Lord may give us is the opportunity to trust his faithfulness during seasons of unanswered prayer. Perhaps you've earnestly prayed for something and have yet to see God move. Or maybe you've lost hope that your prayers have power to change your situation. This verse assures us that God hears and responds to the persistent prayers of his people. It's important to note that he never promised to give us what we want just because we pray really hard; but this Scripture does say that our prayers have great power and will produce wonderful results. Perhaps the "wonderful results" aren't the changing of circumstances but the changing of our hearts. Might God already be answering your earnest prayers in ways that are different from what you expected?

1 Peter 5:7

*Give all your worries and cares to God,
for he cares about you.*

Have you ever shared with a close friend or counselor the concerns that were weighing you down? Was there something healing about verbally processing your worries with someone who cared about you? Sharing your burdens eases the feeling that you need to carry them all on your own. This is also what God wants you to do with him. He longs for you to tell him your burdens, because he cares about you more than any person ever could. Scripture promises that when you release your worries into his control and "thank him for all he has done," he will give you a peace that exceeds your understanding (Philippians 4:6-7). What worries can you talk to God about today?

Psalm 133:1

How wonderful and pleasant it is when brothers live together in harmony!

This verse from Psalms affirms the benefits that come when people live together in unity. Because all of us are sinful, we're bound to face conflict from time to time. But God blesses those who actively work toward unity, peace, and intimacy with others. How do you choose to work through conflict? Do you allow yourself to indulge in gossip, angry words, resentment, and bitterness? Or do you see disagreements as opportunities to deepen your relationships as you actively try to repair what has been torn? Ask God to give you the wisdom and patience to live in harmony with those he has placed in your life.

1 John 3:1

See how very much our Father loves us, for he calls us his children, and that is what we are!

Have you ever felt like you didn't quite belong? Maybe you long to feel more closely tied to a group of friends, better connected at church, or more comfortable within your own family. Jesus promises that when we decide to follow him, we are completely and absolutely a part of his family. We aren't seen as distant family members or sporadic houseguests—God sees us as his beloved *children*. Rest in the truth that no matter what you are feeling, no one and nothing can take your place in his family.

Jude 1:24-25

All glory to God, who is able to keep you from falling away and will bring you with great joy into his glorious presence without a single fault. . . . All glory, majesty, power, and authority are his before all time, and in the present, and beyond all time! Amen.

Jude, one of Jesus' half brothers, closed his letter to the church with this beautiful prayer. It would be a great way to close your day as well. Pray that God will keep your heart in tune with his until he brings you into his presence for eternity. Thank him for his great majesty and for his power and authority over all creation. Praise him that he sees you as his perfect child, without a single fault. He deserves glory for all that he is on this day and on every day that is yet to come.

Revelation 1:8

"I am the Alpha and the Omega—the beginning and the end," says the Lord God. "I am the one who is, who always was, and who is still to come—the Almighty One."

In this passage, "the Alpha and the Omega" refers to the first and last letters of the Greek alphabet. God is the beginning of all creation, and one day he will end creation as we know it, ushering in a new and perfect world for eternity. How should this truth impact the way we live now? Often these "in-between" days feel meaningless, mundane, and lonely. Yet the fact remains that before the beginning of time, God decided to create each and every person for a unique purpose, including you! This gives our lives meaning as we trust his plans for us now and in the future. Live wisely today as you anticipate eternity with him.

Revelation 21:3-4

Look, God's home is now among his people!
He will live with them, and they will be his people.
God himself will be with them. He will wipe every
tear from their eyes, and there will be no more
death or sorrow or crying or pain. All these things
are gone forever.

This passage holds some of the most comforting promises for those who are grieving. One day, our home will finally be with God. He will live among us in a place where there is no more death, sorrow, crying, or pain. Can you even imagine it? What might it feel like to never be afraid or sad again? Be encouraged knowing that one day you'll live in perfect peace in God's heavenly Kingdom, where grief will be gone forever.

Scripture Index